MARY FROST:

WIFE,

MOTHER,

CHARTIST

Sylvia Mason

with a foreword by
Jayne Bryant MS/ΛS

Published by Saron Publishing in 2022

ISBN-13: paperback: 978-1-913297-27-5
e-book: 978-1-913297-28-2

Saron Publishers
Pwllmeyrick House
Mamhilad
Mon
NP4 8RG

saronpublishers.co.uk
info@saronpublishers.co.uk
Follow us on Facebook and Twitter

For
Olwen, Dilys and Annabella

Also by Sylvia Mason

Every Woman Remembered

Acknowledgements

I was helped and advised by many people in writing this account. I thank them all most sincerely.

The Our Chartist Heritage group whose knowledge of - and enthusiasm for - the events surrounding the Newport Rising are unrivalled, has been an invaluable source of information. The input of David Osmond, Pat Drewett, Melinda Drowley, Sarah Richards, Les James and Ray Stroud has been very much appreciated.

Thanks to three longstanding friends: Janet Tyson who was able to suggest a new perspective, Ann Hopkins, again, loaned me books from her extensive collection, and Jayne Bryant who, despite her demanding role representing Newport West in the Welsh Parliament, found time to read the book and write the Foreword. Thanks, too, to Enrico Rovelli, in Milan, who took a real interest in researching Italian websites, and sourced documents from his contacts in Palermo University. Also to Janice Williams who translated, from 19th century ecclesiastical Italian, the long and tricky handwritten marriage records of Sarah Frost.

Derek Butler drew the plan of Newport for which I am more than grateful.

I also wish to acknowledge the help given by Eva Taylor, Archives Assistant at Bristol Archives, Colin Gibson of Gwent Archives, Robert Lawrence of the Bristol and Avon Family History Society and the staff at Newport Reference Library.

My friends in the Newport Women's Forum, led by Dame Rosemary Butler, have given me so much encouragement and support.

I value the friendly, professional and fuss-free approach of Penny Reeves at Saron Publishers and thank her again for all her assistance.

I remain, as ever, thankful for my husband, Colin.

Sylvia Mason
Newport
January 2022

Proceeds from the sale of this book will be divided between two very worthy charities: The Newport Women's Forum and Our Chartist Heritage.

Newport Women's Forum

The Newport Women's Forum Bursary award began in 1996. A group of women had their savings boosted when their building society became a bank. They decided to put that money to good use and support other women. Since then, the Forum has offered an annual bursary to help women achieve their dreams. Former winners include a grandmother who, after a lifetime of writing poetry, was awarded the funds to publish her work; a student, given a grant to undertake a Voluntary Service Overseas placement in Nigeria; and a group of women, financed to attend a weekend outward bound confidence-building course.

The Forum is led by founding member Dame Rosemary Butler. Funds are raised by women for women, through donations, our annual International Women's Day Celebration, and smaller fund-raising events such as coffee mornings and teas held in our members' and supporters' homes and gardens. We are delighted and thank Sylvia that she has once again decided to support NWF through sharing the proceeds of her second excellent book, which highlights yet another hidden heroine of Newport, Mary Frost.

To find out more please contact us via:
Website: NewportWF.Wordpress.com
Email: NewportWomensForum@gmail.com
Facebook: Newport Women's Forum
Twitter: @NewportWomen
Jeanette Hawrot, Administrator

Our Chartist Heritage

The publication of Sylvia Mason's book about Mary Frost has been eagerly anticipated by Our Chartist Heritage (OCH), especially members of the Chartist Women's Group and the specialist historians who organise the annual Chartist Convention.

OCH is small, grass-roots charity based in Newport, South Wales. Our purpose is to provide education for the public benefit in the history and heritage of the Chartist movement. In 2021, some of us take for granted the rights for which the Chartists fought, while others of us still feel disenfranchised and silenced in so many different ways. For these reasons, we are committed to promoting and defending Article 21 of the Universal Declaration of Human Rights, which affirms the right of all to participate in the government of their country and civic life.

One of the challenges of writing about the 1839 Newport Rising is the necessity of contending with what David Jones (1986) describes as the 'secret and baffling nature of the evidence'. Sylvia has bravely taken on an additional challenge by focusing on the hidden and largely undocumented life of one of the women situated at the centre of a story that is normally populated exclusively by male protagonists.

OCH aims to enable people to make meaningful connections between the events that took place in Newport in 1839 and their lives as citizens today. Without compromising any of the integrity of her biographical historical research, Sylvia achieves precisely this by enriching her study of Mary Frost with insights and inferences from contemporary literary sources and other illuminating contextual material. Her approach is suggestive rather than didactic, gently inviting readers to join her in making imaginative and creative connections with Mary Frost's life and times.

OCH is honoured to be associated with this publication and immensely grateful to Sylvia for generously donating half the proceeds of this new book to support our work.

Dr Melinda Drowley
Chair of Board of Trustees | Our Chartist Heritage
www.newportrising.co.uk
www.our-chartist-heritage.co.uk

Foreword

History isn't just about key events or dates - it's about people. Generally women have been defined in history by their role as mothers, wives, sisters and daughters. Stories of struggle, courage and success have not been heard or passed down. Their voices lost like whispers in the wind. Some we will never hear again, but others can be amplified. Sylvia Mason has sought out these voices by researching local women who led extraordinary lives that are too often overlooked. In this book, she poses questions which allow the reader to think what might have happened at crucial times. With attention to detail, Sylvia hooks you in to a time and place which adds to our understanding of a significant time in Newport's history. An event which reverberated around Wales and the rest of the UK.

For many years on 4th November, people have gathered in St Woolos Cathedral graveyard to commemorate and remember the Chartist cause and the tragic events of the Newport Rising of 1839. Until relatively recently, the only mention of women were of those who said goodbye to their loved ones before the march or mourned for their loss. The names that we know are mostly those of the women who have family connections to prominent Chartists. So many others remain lost to history.

Sylvia has brought to life Mary Frost and the struggles she faced as part of the Chartist movement, both before and after the Uprising. She has opened the door on the family life of Mary and her children and the challenges she had to navigate. Thanks to Sylvia's descriptions, the book makes you feel like an eyewitness to some of the pivotal moments, evoking the volatility of Mary's 19th century Newport life. It was a Newport that was growing rapidly and a vignette for the social divides across Britain at that time. It had 5,500 residents but only 80 voters. Vast unelected power ran rife, serving an elite few, unchecked by democratic processes. John Frost did not take on this democratic deficit alone, but without Mary alongside, it is unlikely that he would have been the man we remember today.

I hope you enjoy reading this as much as I did. Sylvia has given Mary Frost her voice.

Jayne Bryant
Member of the Senedd
Aelodau o'r Senedd

Mary's Family

Uncle
William Foster, Mary's mother's brother, 1755-1820
Margaret Foster, nee Rosser, his wife, Mary's aunt, 1750-1829

First husband
Charles Geach, 1780-1807

Children with Charles Geach
William Foster Geach, 1804 or 1805, married Elizabeth Williams
Mary Foster Geach, 1806, married George Lawrence

Second husband
John Frost, 1785-1877

Mother-in-law
Sarah Roberts, previously Frost and Jones, nee Waters, 1760-1851

Children with John Frost
John Frost, 1813
Elizabeth Frost, 1815
Sarah Mary Frost, 1817, married Harry Fry and Guiseppe Pasqualino
Catharine Frost, 1818
Ellen Frost, 1820, married William Davies
Henry Hunt Frost, 1822–1842
James Frost, 1824–1825
Anne Frost, 1826

Grandchildren from both her marriages

Herbert Henry Geach, 1831
Mary Lawrence, 1832
Elizabeth Lawrence, 1833
John Lawrence, 1835
Anne Lawrence, 1837
Henrietta Lawrence, 1838
Helen Louisa Foster, 1839
Dennis Fitzroy Kelly Fry, 1839
Fanny Mary Fry, 1842
Ellen Anne Davies, 1843
Emilia Pasquelino, 1861

Mary was a quiet, modest woman, a woman who kept herself in the background. She was described as a lady by birth, education and fortune.[1] But it was her qualities of strength and resilience which were essential for her to survive all the devastating events which lay before her.

Until now, her life, like that of so many women, remained a sub-plot; unexamined and undervalued.

Plan of Newport — not to scale

Baneswell

Stow Hill

Pentonville

55 b

B

Commercial St

High St

Friars
Fields

C

E

Wharves

River Usk

Rodney Parade

Key
A St Woolos
B Westgate Hotel
C Hope Chapel
D Thomas St
E King's Head Hotel

This drawing of Newport was printed in Pigot's Directory of 1835.
St Woolos (now Newport) Cathedral can be seen at the top of the
hill.

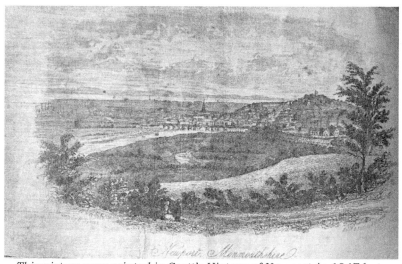

This picture was printed in Scott's History of Newport in 1847 but
is clearly of an earlier date, possibly the late 1700s before the
construction of the stone bridge. Stow Hill can be seen leading
uphill to St Woolos (now Newport) Cathedral.

CHAPTER 1

1782-1811

Mary Morgan was born in Monmouthshire in 1782,[2] into a world very different from our own. While she was small, Mary probably played, as other girls, with wooden and cloth dolls, toys and games, and read the children's picture books available at that time. She would have worn smaller versions of adult clothes with a pinafore over her dresses during the day. When she was old enough, she would have attended school, quite possibly boarding school. At the end of the 18th century, a girl's education could be thorough but gender specific. Reading was popular and although books were expensive, in many towns it was possible to join a circulating library. No woman could hope to attend university or enter a profession. Middle-class girls and women like Mary would spend their time usefully, reading, writing, sewing, painting and practising music. They were occupied with family responsibilities and philanthropic work.

If exploring the lives of women of the past, like Mary, were only attempted when the historical record is full, so many interesting women would be ignored - and our history would be the poorer. Because the documented record generally has little interest in ordinary women, attempts to reconstruct their lives have to been done imaginatively. Mary was not aristocratic, scandalous, fabulously wealthy or talented, so her imprint on the written record is light, but it is enough. Because novels of the time often give us a clearer picture of women's lives than history books, this account attempts to be true to the historical events while, from time to time, using references to the great literature of the period to portray the interesting life of this Newport woman, her daughters and friends.

Jane Austen, that great observer of provincial life and the subtleties of class and gender, had been born seven years earlier, in 1775. Mary's worldview would have been in some ways similar to that described in Jane Austen's novels, as the lives of Austen's female characters reflect those of her class and generation. The women are economically dependent, second-class citizens whose lives revolve around home and family. Most have received the education prescribed for females - literacy skills, instruction in ornamental accomplishments and manners. The main objective of this education was to attract a husband and reinforce the docile feminine qualities admired by men. This was the education provided, for example, for tradesman's daughter Harriet Smith, at Mrs Goddard's school in Jane Austen's novel *Emma*. Most women, therefore, unless they were financially independent, often had only one real ambition - to marry and, preferably, marry well. Marriage was the only way for them to obtain independence from their parents, gain their own home, some status and respect, and avoid the stigma of 'spinsterhood'. Such would probably have been the influences in Mary's early life.

Quite early on, like Austen's female characters, she would have realised that being a girl meant her life was destined to be restricted by her gender, and that she had to conform to traditional roles. She would have realised that men were in control of society and that she would have little say in the circumstances of her own life, let alone the wider world. Female inferiority in Regency times was seen as a natural law. The almost universal acceptance of the 'two spheres' idea meant that marriage, motherhood and housekeeping were the destiny of middle-class women like Mary. Only within the home did women have power and moral influence. Also accepted were the double standards which applied to the conduct of men and women. Mary Wollstonecraft, another female writer, was pioneering a more ambitious life for women. Perhaps Mary Morgan read *The Vindication of the Rights of Women,* published in 1792, as it was very widely available. The letters Mary wrote later in her life show she was intelligent and highly literate.

Owning land was the main form of wealth in the 18th century. In Mary's world, political power and influence were in the hands of rich landowners: both political parties, the Whigs and the Tories, were composed of aristocrats. At the summit of society was the nobility. Below them were landowners called the gentry. The rights to vote and to stand for public office were denied to most people. In the Newport area, the Morgan family, who owned Tredegar House and would later become the Lords of Tredegar, wielded immense political power and influence and they gave power to their favourites, associates and employees.

At this period, however, people such as merchants and professional men were becoming richer and more numerous, especially in towns. They were increasingly able to become involved in the political scene. Mary's family was of this affluent middle class. She was part of a comfortably off Newport family.

She was born when the Industrial Revolution was beginning to transform people's lives. The growing industrialisation of the Welsh valleys, with iron works and coal mining, meant wealth for Newport, changing forever this small market town because of the strategic importance of its rapidly expanding maritime trade. It was becoming one of the largest towns in Wales. For the workers, men, women and children, enticed from their rural lives to service these heavy industries, life was anything but comfortable. Governance was still essentially feudal, with landowners and the new industrialists exercising absolute power to their own advantage. Radical political persons and ideas which threatened this status quo were dealt with very severely by the powers that be.

Newport had been a little market town, almost rural in nature, with a population of about a thousand in 1800. The main street led from the river bridge through High Street and up Stow Hill to St Woolos Church. Only two streets were paved, High Street and Commercial Street. The rapid industrialisation of the valleys north of Newport, however, led to a newly constructed canal and a tramroad to bring the iron and coal down to Newport. The town grew to provide buildings for the expanding population to live and work. Houses of the poor were often overcrowded and unhealthy but there was money to be made.

One man who was to play a crucial role in Mary's life was her uncle, William Foster, her mother's brother. He was a wealthy merchant in Newport and a builder, owning many properties in Newport and Cardiff. He was involved in local politics and was appointed alderman in 1803 and was mayor of the town in 1804 and again in 1812 and 1817.[3] In 1789, he had married Margaret Rosser who was also destined to play her part in Mary's life.

On 29th September 1803, fulfilling her traditional destiny, Mary married.[4] Her husband was Charles

Geach. They were nonconformists and Parliament at that time required most nonconformists to be married by Anglican ministers. The ceremony took place at St Woolos Church in Newport as they were both living in the parish. She would have promised to obey her husband as part of her wedding vows. The witnesses were her uncle, William Foster, and C Morgan who may well have been one of her Morgan relatives. So Mary Morgan left girlhood behind and became Mrs Charles Geach and a new stage in her life began. She had her own home to run and a different status in society, but it was a life in which she was still dependent on a man, a man who had power over her. If anything, marriage confirmed her subordinate position. Any property she owned was from then on controlled and managed by him.

Charles was just two years her senior and a timber merchant by profession. His business probably revolved around the importing of wood through Newport to provide pit props and other items necessary in the coal mines. Wood was also in high demand for the Navy and required for all the housing and other building work which was going on apace in Newport and the surrounding area for the expanding population. He was a prosperous man.

Charles and Mary's first child, a son, was born, probably, the following year. They named him William.[5] Two years later she gave birth to a daughter, Mary, named after herself. Little Mary was baptised on 15th May 1806 in the Wesleyan Ebenezer Chapel. The name 'Foster' was added to William's and Mary's names sometime before adulthood.

Pregnancy could be hazardous. There were no anaesthetics and women sometimes died in childbirth. Infant mortality was high. Lack of hygiene was a huge problem in Newport as in other towns. People relied on

St Woolos Church, now Newport Cathedral
photo taken in 2020
The plaque which commemorates the Chartists killed in the Rising
can be seen on the wall on the left.

wells for their water and the public wells were polluted, especially in Baneswell, causing diseases such as typhoid, diphtheria and cholera. Tuberculosis was prevalent, too. Mary would have done all she could to protect her children but when tragedy struck, it was not the death of a child but the death of her husband. Charles Geach died in 1807.[6] Mary went into mourning. After just four years of marriage, at twenty-five years of age, with two babies, Mary was a widow. A wealthy widow.

She and her children were taken in by her childless uncle and aunt, William and Margaret Foster. The Fosters were rich, influential and fond of her, and both being in their fifties, had no hope of children of their own. She became the nearest person to their own child. Her life would have been warm and comfortable. She could watch her children, William and Mary, grow and prosper, a consolation in her grief. She had inherited money from Charles and there was the expectation that she and her children would inherit the Fosters' wealth, too.

Five years later, she made an amazing, destiny-changing decision. She could have been expected to make an advantageous second marriage but instead she chose a young man of little property who ran a draper's shop on High Street. And so it is that at this point, we move out of the world of Jane Austen and into the wider world like that described by Charles Dickens, Elizabeth Gaskell and George Eliot, into a world of riches and poverty, of powerful elites and a powerless underclass with a middle class straddling the two.

St David's Church, Bettws, where Mary married John Frost
Photos taken in 2021

CHAPTER 2

1812-1819

On 24th October 1812, Mary married for a second time. The wedding took place in the Parish Church at Bettws, a mile or two north of Newport, as Mary was living in that parish. As she made her vows, 'for better, for worse, for richer, for poorer...', she cannot have imagined what lay ahead. On this occasion, neither C Morgan nor William Foster were witnesses. In contrast with Charles Geach, of whom we know very little, there is almost too much information about her new husband, John Frost. He assumed centre stage in her life and often, in the many accounts of this charismatic man, it is tantalisingly difficult to glimpse Mary. But these glimpses we have of her, though infrequent, are enough for a reader with imagination to flesh out a life.

Her new husband, John, like her, was from a Newport family. His parents John and Sarah had been married at St Woolos in 1782 and he, their only surviving child, was born in 1785. Less than two years later, his father died. He had been an innkeeper of the public house he owned, The Royal Oak in Thomas Street, just off High Street. This was left to young John although his mother ran it for most of her long life. John was brought up by his grandfather, a bootmaker, and his grandmother. He left Newport to pursue a career in Cardiff and then Bristol, furnished with letters of recommendation from William Foster, who was then an alderman in the town and to whom he was distantly related. He also spent some time in London. John was bookish, highly intelligent, very literate – good-looking, too, with a kindly expression. In the *Charter*, he was described as 'gentlemanly'.[7] He was interested in religion and, like Mary, was a non-conformist. He was also attracted to local politics.

When John had returned to Newport in 1806, he had been given premises at 55 High Street to start a drapery business by William Roberts, a man who was to become his stepfather, his widowed mother's third husband. In Newport lived many of his extended family: aunts, uncles and cousins. His mother kept the Royal Oak just a few minutes' walk away. It was to this draper's shop and extended family that he brought Mary on their marriage. The business was successful and so she became a comfortably off, tradesman's wife. She was no longer part of the higher reaches of Newport society as perhaps she could have been, but there is no doubt she loved John dearly and he her. He had chosen well for she was not only rich but a quiet and loyal wife. He was twenty-eight, she was thirty, and they were happy.

The typical firm in the 19th century was a small family partnership which meant many opportunities existed for wives and daughters to be actively involved. There is evidence of their important roles, mostly behind the scenes: in retailing, dealing with clients, correspondence, bookkeeping, arranging deals. A role in the bustling world of commerce sounds more fulfilling for Mary than life in a lady's drawing room. At that time, a linen draper often draped selected fabrics across the doorway so they could be seen and felt. It could be a lucrative business as there were enough wealthy people around who wanted expensive fabrics for tablecloths, bed linen and so on, and since ready-to-wear clothes were not readily available until the mid-19th century, drapers were in great demand by seamstresses and tailors. Often people bought cloth and made their own clothes.

At a time when there were no department stores or supermarkets, a high street would have individual shops, each selling a specified type of product. Newport had its rows of diverse shops selling whatever the citizens of the town and surrounding area required. People usually shopped for their fresh food every day. Market day in Newport was Saturday so this would have been the busiest time. There was no market building in High Street at that time until one was built in 1817, so market stalls were set up in the street. The monthly cattle markets would have filled High Street with animals, leaving the shopkeepers to clean the mess from outside their premises. In bi-lingual Newport, Welsh would have been the preferred language of some of the customers, especially those coming from the valleys. High Street was a bustling and prosperous part of town with offices, inns, shops, banks and hotels. Near them, at 65 High Street, was Napper's Muffin Shop, famed for its gingerbread. It became a meeting place for the wealthier citizens. Did John and Mary enjoy Napper's gingerbread? I hope so.

Near them also, was an office of Charles Morgan of Tredegar Park. The rapid expansion of Newport meant land became much more profitable and the person to benefit most from this was Charles Morgan. Working in this office as his Estate Manager was a young lawyer from Usk, Thomas Prothero, who had managed to find favour with Charles Morgan. The Frosts could hardly have predicted that the young man they must have seen about on High Street would come to play such a huge role in their lives. Prothero, ambitious and ruthless, soon began managing the estates of other great landlords in Monmouthshire as well as securing various other public appointments. He became, in later years, extremely powerful and hugely influential in the affairs of the town. The Frosts would have watched, dismayed and disgusted, as this unprincipled man moved upwards, from poverty and his rented room in Thomas Street, living first in the Friars on Belle Vue Lane and then in Malpas Court.[8] He was John's absolute opposite. John was popular as he and Mary were known for their kindness and fair dealing, whereas Prothero was hated and feared. Prothero was to become John's nemesis.

The Frosts' first child was born on 8th October 1813. They named him John after his father. He was baptised on 4th November at Hope Chapel. This was a church of Protestant dissenters of the Independent denomination, later to become Congregationalists, who rejected the hierarchical structures of other denominations. They had no bishops nor elders and they rejected the role of the state in religious matters. They believed in freedom of conscience. Each autonomous community was self-governing, and authority rested with the people, who appointed and paid their own ministers. It is easy to see the appeal of radical politics to those who were committed to this form of religious allegiance. Hope Chapel in Newport had been built before 1810 and enlarged by 1814. It was in Chapel Row at the back of Commercial Street, almost opposite the Westgate Hotel. Both Mary and John were devout and this was their place of worship throughout their time in Newport. Through good times and bad, Mary would have said her prayers and read her bible.

After John, Mary gave birth to three daughters: Elizabeth on 18th March 1815, Sarah on 16th January 1817 and Catharine on 16th October 1818. All were baptised at Hope Chapel and the celebration for Sarah's baptism on 16th February 1817 was held on the same day as the marriage of John's mother Sarah to William

Roberts, her third and final husband. Sarah had clearly been named after her grandmother.

Throughout this time, John's political ideas had been developing along radical lines and he began to focus on the corruption of those in power in Newport, where, as in the country as a whole, an unrepresentative elite were able to strengthen the hands of the rich against the poor. There can be little doubt that Mary shared his views. By this time, John was a freeholder and burgess and, like William Foster, interested in local politics as a means of bringing about change. Did he still meet with William Foster's approval? This seems unlikely. John's friends were amongst the radicals of Newport like Samuel Etheridge, the printer. The *Cambrian* newspaper on 1st August 1818 carried an advertisement for tickets for a dinner at the Parrot Inn in Newport. The guest of honour was to be Charles Morgan and the invitation was extended to 'Gentlemen friendly to the House of Tredegar'. William Foster was to be in the chair. He clearly aligned himself with the gentry. John was certainly no friend of the Morgans.

On 16th August 1819, the most famous radical orator of the day, Henry Hunt, was speaking at a meeting of 80,000 people at St Peter's Field in Manchester. His topic was the urgently needed parliamentary reform. Local magistrates ordered the yeomanry, the volunteer part-time cavalry, to break up the meeting. They charged the crowd, killing eleven people and injuring many more. It became known as the Peterloo Massacre. Henry Hunt was arrested and subsequently imprisoned for two and a half years. Without doubt, the Frosts' sympathies would have been with Hunt and the unarmed protesters. They, too, believed parliamentary reform was necessary so that laws would benefit the poor as well as the rich. They also believed in the right of peaceful protest to achieve this.

31

CHAPTER 3

1820-1823

As the new decade started in 1820, Mary's personal life must have felt settled. She had a kind and intelligent husband who was a good businessman. They had a growing family, rich relations and a network of friends and acquaintances through the shop and their membership of Hope Chapel. They deplored the inequalities in society and the corrupt administration in Newport but had the energy and the will to fight these. But just two months into the new decade, on Leap Year's Day 1820, Mary's uncle, William Foster, the man who had been like a father to her, died aged sixty-five. Mary again put on her mourning clothes. He was buried at St Woolos on 5th March.

His complicated will, which had been drawn up by Thomas Prothero, left all his wealth to his widow, Margaret, in the first instance, with money in trust for the education of William and Mary Foster Geach.[9] This was a terrible blow. John and Mary must have been bitterly disappointed as they had expectations of inheriting his considerable fortune. They would have nothing until Margaret Foster's death or remarriage. At that point, his wealth was to be split three ways between William and Mary Foster Geach, and Mary Frost. But in the latter case, Mary Frost's portion was to be tied up in a way which ensured John would not be able to access it. The actual wording of this clause in his will is:

To the extent that the same may not be at the disposal of or subject to or liable to the control forfeiture debts or engagements of the said John Frost her husband, or any future husband she may marry, but only at her sole and separate disposal for and during the term of her natural life.

And so started the feud between the Frosts and Margaret Foster's lawyer, the pugilistic Thomas Prothero, possibly, by then, the most powerful man in Newport. All John's political struggles became linked to this personal feud.

We can only guess what Mary's feelings about this were. She knew her uncle much better than John. He had taken her and her children into his home when Charles Geach died, and she had given them his name. Her expectation of inheriting his wealth must have sprung from some indication from him. She would have been aware before his death that William Foster disapproved of her husband, but she could not help being shocked at this disavowing of his care for her. What was probably perceived by William Foster was that John's reformist views were also shared by her, for his will not only prevented John from benefitting but any other husband Mary might have. The implication is that if Mary were to marry again, she would choose another radical, someone of whom William Foster would have disapproved. Of course, it has always been assumed that John's radicalism influenced her but it could have been the other way about. It would explain why in 1812 she was living in Bettws, which was then not part of Newport, and why her uncle was not a witness at her second marriage.

The disappointment at William Foster's will was the first of all the setbacks and tragedies that would result from their political radicalism. The men who held all the power would tolerate no threat to their established positions. But similar political views to theirs were held by many. Radical literature of the time was freely available and they would certainly have discussed Paine's *Rights of Man*. June 1820 saw the publication of Volume 1 of Henry Hunt's *Memoirs*, written while he was serving his prison sentence. This again was essential reading.

On 17th July, Margaret Foster drafted a new will leaving everything to Mary's daughter, Mary Foster Geach, who was aged fourteen and living with her at the time. It did not revoke the provisos of her late husband's will. This must have upset the Frosts, especially John. He again blamed Prothero, Margaret's lawyer. But Prothero was a force to be reckoned with in Newport for he was protected by Charles Morgan. With this patronage, he could ruthlessly advance his own career, becoming richer and more powerful at every opportunity. Doubtless, the anger John felt towards Prothero was shared by Mary.

But for Mary, life in the shop and bringing up her young family must have occupied most of her time and energy and less than two years after the birth of Catharine, Mary gave birth to another daughter. Ellen was born on 17th September 1820. They seem to have been in no rush to baptise their latest child as Ellen's baptism was delayed until 17th December. Mary was thirty-eight. Was she taking longer to recover from the births of her children? Or did they have other things on their minds?

John was now producing pamphlets which excoriated Thomas Prothero, accusing him of sharp practice, hypocrisy and extortion. Was Mary becoming aware and anxious that her husband's anger and resentment could start to damage their livelihood and family? Many citizens of Newport were delighted that Prothero was being exposed but Prothero was not the man to take this lying down. He wanted revenge. Mary must have been shocked and horrified when, in January 1821, John was arrested at Prothero's instigation and charged with libel. At one point, he was kept in custody in his own home for thirty-six hours by the town constables. How distressing this would have been for Mary and the children. Having the police standing sentry outside was, at the very least, unsettling and embarrassing. The children can hardly have understood it. But the sufferings caused to the family by John's actions had hardly begun.

The case was heard in Middlesex, a long way from John's friends and supporters in Monmouthshire. Mary, who was pregnant again, prayed and waited anxiously to hear the verdict. She would also have had to run the shop on her own. When John arrived back in Newport on Tuesday 5th March, he had a huge welcome from his friends. His great popularity in the town must have cheered the family. But John was almost ruined financially. This was a terrible setback for them. What had happened to the money Mary had brought to the marriage? It would have been John's to administer so perhaps it was used in developing the business and all now lost. What could Mary do but protect the children and support John?

On 13th August 1822, John and Thomas Prothero again went to court, this time in Monmouth. Prothero was able to pack the jury with his supporters so, unsurprisingly, John was found guilty. He sold all the stock from their shop to pay his debts except £200 (approximately £12,000 today)[10] he owed to his stepfather, William Roberts, who had him arrested. It is clear John was trying to get himself declared bankrupt and his mother and stepfather were aiding him in this. But from Mary's point of view, this was a family disaster. She had given birth to their second son less than a fortnight before. Henry Hunt Frost was born on 1st August 1822 and proudly named for the great radical orator of Peterloo. This was an act of defiance which made clear to all where their allegiance lay. But with a tiny baby, five small children, a shop without stock and a bankrupt husband, Mary was at a low point in her life. John even instructed her to sell some of their furniture.

The only ray of light in the terrible situation was that the bankruptcy appears to have been a put-up job by his stepfather to protect the rest of the Frosts' assets. Sadly, this plan was not successful. Friends helped to support him and his family when, on 28th August 1822, he was imprisoned in Monmouth Gaol. He spent his time improving his Welsh, reading and writing and apparently having a comfortable time.[11] He sent a letter to Mary regarding the arrangements for transferring ownership of the shop to their son John. Mary's life was grim. She was in effect a single mother, and a single mother with no money to support herself and her children. She would have needed as much help as she could get. This was all a far cry from her earlier, simpler, more comfortable life.

Ironically, Henry Hunt was released from prison in the very month, October, that John's release from prison was opposed by Prothero. Mary then knew he would have to spend a further six months in gaol, and that she would have to manage without him. Their network of relatives and friends supported her and the children through this terrible time.

On 26th October 1822, the following was printed in Samuel Etheridge's radical paper, the *Newport Review*:

> *The friends of Mr Frost who have subscribed towards the support of him and his family during*

his imprisonment will meet at the Royal Oak on Monday night and continue to meet for that purpose once a fortnight.

She could never have imagined at the beginning of her married life with John that she would become a recipient of public charity and a subject of pity. Much of the trauma could not have been kept from the older children. John, then aged just nine, would have been quite old enough to have sensed any difference in his mother's usual mood, but perhaps not old enough to understand the political views of his parents. Nor, maybe, his mother's loyalty to his father. The minister, Jenkin Lewis, and congregation of Hope Chapel would have been another source of help, as her faith was so important to her. Mary would have been distressed that she had to have little Henry baptised without the presence of his proud father. Henry Hunt Frost was baptised on 3rd November by Jenkin Lewis in Hope Chapel just like his siblings. I hope Mary was granted some joy that day.

Did her aunt Margaret Foster come to her aid? This is possible, for at that time she was making arrangements in Bristol, where she was living, to secure the future of Mary's eldest son. On 21st December 1822, with the support of his aunt, William Foster Geach was articled to a solicitor in Bristol. He was to train and then practise in Bristol. This was something Mary could not have done for him so her aunt's actions must have been a consolation at the end of a terrible year. She would have been pleased he was settled - and settle he did and went on to qualify as a very able and energetic solicitor, practising in Bristol until 1830. Bristol was a tactful choice for William's training in view of John's dispute with at least one influential firm of solicitors in Newport, as William would have been known locally as John's stepson.

The new year of 1823 brought little relief for the Frosts. On 3rd February, John was transferred from Monmouth Gaol to the Marshalsea in London. The prison became well-known in the 19th century through the works of writer Charles Dickens, whose father was imprisoned there for a debt of forty pounds and ten shillings in 1824 when the novelist was twelve years old. The experience deeply affected Dickens and the imprisonment of debtors in the Marshalsea prison is a frequent theme in his novels, especially *Little Dorrit* and *The Pickwick Papers*. Families could visit the prison; indeed, families could lodge there and often needed to if they had no other home.[12] The prison was privately run and charged for food and other essentials so John would have needed his family and friends to send him money. There is no record of the Frost family having visited and John did not expect to be there long as he was hoping soon to be returned to Monmouth.

Mary must have been bitterly disappointed and dismayed when his request was not only refused but the decision taken that he was to be transferred on 11th February 1823 to Cold Bath Fields, London, where the conditions were terrible. Cold Bath Fields, built in 1794 on a swamp, had a reputation for severity. The most dangerous criminals were often lodged there before being transferred to the Tower or transported to Australia. He was there for six months. A terrible time for him, but also a terrible time for Mary and the children. She must have relied heavily on her Christian faith as well as her friends.

To Mary's relief, John survived his ordeal and returned home. He was ordered to pay £500 (over £28,000 today) as security for his good behaviour for five years. He arrived back in Newport in triumph, met by crowds of supporters with banners and a band playing,

See the Conquering Hero Come.[13] What did Mary think? She had had to take responsibility for the children and the business alone while he had been away for the best part of a year. Did he accept how hard it must have been for her? Despite how much she agreed with his political radicalism, however much she loved him, did she never wonder about her choice of husband? She admired his energetic, confident, ambitious personality but it was so very different from her own careful, retiring nature.

CHAPTER 4

1824-1831

Perhaps it was not only the forfeit of his £500 that kept him quiet for the next few years but also an awareness of his responsibilities as a husband and father. Were there tears and words said in private? Whatever the reason, Mary would have been encouraged when he set about putting his affairs in order. He was an excellent businessman and the drapers shop again prospered in the centre of the rapidly enlarging and prospering town. Life for the family improved. Their elder daughters, Elizabeth and Sarah, were probably at school by this time. In Newport there were two academies for girls which took both boarding and day pupils: a school run by Miss King and the other in Commercial Street by the Misses Thomas.[14] The Frost girls could have been sent away to school, of course, as some of their friends were.[15] We know they were well educated.

By the end of 1823, Mary was pregnant again and she gave birth to James on 7th August the following year. They waited four months to have little James baptised which suggests they had no fear for his life. Non-conformists did not think baptism was efficacious in the way High Anglicans did, but they clearly thought it important. It was not until 12th December 1824, that James was baptised in Hope Chapel by Jenkin Lewis, just like the other children. But James died within a few weeks, in January 1825. This was a great tragedy just when it seemed Mary's life had taken a better turn. Her grief can be imagined as it cast a shadow over the future. But life went on around her and Mary, even in her sadness, was a woman who did her duty. She had a place to fill and a job to do. The other children were growing up and the shop was doing well.[16] Improvements were being made in the town, too, as more roads were being surfaced and gas lighting was installed along the streets.

The number and variety of shops was increasing. By 1830 there would be more than sixty individual shops on High Street alone, as well as the Post Office, banks, offices and hotels.[17] It was a bustling area and people had money to spend.

Mary's final child, a girl, was born on 1st July 1826. Mary was forty-four. She had given birth to at least ten children and, as far as we know, all but one had survived. They named their newest arrival Anne, and she was baptised on 6th August. There followed then for Mary a few uneventful years. John's radical political views had by no means altered but during these years he was keeping a lower public profile. The family saw more of him and felt more settled.

There was some good news: Mary's eldest son, William, who was still in Bristol, qualified as a solicitor in February 1828 and began his practice in that city. And there was some bad news: William Roberts, husband of Mary's mother-in-law Sarah Roberts, died in 1829, leaving her a widow for the third time. The family again went into mourning. He had been a good friend to John, helping him when he first returned to Newport in 1806 and again in his legal fight with Prothero in 1822. Sarah remained at the Royal Oak in Thomas Street.

More unsettling for the Frosts was the death of Aunt Margaret Foster on 14th August 1829, aged seventy-nine.[18] She, too, had been living near them on High

Street at that time although the announcement of her death in the *Cheltenham Chronicle* states that she was 'late of Gloucester Street, Bristol'.[19] Her funeral was held at St Woolos on 19th August and her will was approved on 28th May 1830.[20] Her status in Newport can be judged by the inclusion of her name in the list of the gentry in the trade directories. Upon her death Mary's two eldest children, those by her first husband Charles Geach, became very wealthy. It could be thought that such favouritism towards the children of Mary's first marriage would have split the family but this appears not to have been so. At this time, too, Mary, also a beneficiary, would have received her inheritance, giving her a measure of financial security.

As John and Mary's older relatives were dying, the younger ones were growing up and becoming adults. William Foster Geach, then twenty-six, was, thanks to his aunt, a wealthy professional. His sister Mary, too, at twenty-four, was a rich, highly eligible young woman. They wasted no time. Mary was the first to marry. On 7th October 1830 at St Woolos, she married George Lawrence and moved from Newport to her husband's parish of Trevethin, near Pontypool.[21] George Lawrence owned land in Pontnewynydd and was a tanner and a gentleman farmer. Elizabeth Frost was one of the witnesses at the wedding ceremony, suggesting there was no hard feeling between these half-sisters because one had such good fortune.

Just two months later in December 1830, the marriage took place between William Foster Geach and Elizabeth Williams in Trevethin Church. She was from a wealthy county family who expected to inherit money from her rich cousin, Rachel Herbert. William began to move into more exalted social circles. He moved from Bristol to Pontypool where he set up a highly successful solicitor's practice and lived in a great deal of luxury. Politically, he disagreed with his radical parents as he appears to have been a Tory.

That very month, December 1830, when Mary was adjusting to being the mother of married children, John's political silence ended. Could this be linked to the added financial security gained through Mary's inheritance? John acquired the printing equipment of his long-time friend and fellow radical, Samuel Etheridge, and quickly started producing pamphlets. His political views were unchanged. In Newport in 1830, only about eighty of the 5,500 inhabitants were entitled to vote.[22] This was a glaring injustice. John believed that only parliamentary reform could put an end to the inequitable, corrupt British political system. Only when Parliament was elected by the people could all the social ills be dealt with.

He was not alone. All over the country, there were cries for reform. The hardships of the working people became more than many could bear. In August 1831, there was a rising in Merthyr when workers held a town and the military at bay for the best part of a week. Dic Penderyn - Richard Lewis - was hanged in Cardiff Gaol on 13th August. Elizabeth Morgan Howells, the sister of Dic Penderyn, would have been known to the Frosts for she was married to Morgan Howells, the minister of Ebenezer Chapel in Commercial Street.[23] They can have had no doubt about the punishment meted out to leaders of those who militantly challenged the status quo.

In October 1831, they would have had news of the terrible Bristol riot. In fact, according to the report in the *Monmouthshire Merlin*, Newport people saw it with their own eyes, as, in the early hours of Monday 31st October 1831, a massive crowd gathered at Newport Bridge to view the flames of Bristol burning in the night sky. Many Bristol civilians were killed by the soldiers and in the fires. At least eight-six were wounded by sword cuts or horses' hooves. Civil unrest was on the rise.

That was the year that Mary learned she was to become a grandmother. Elizabeth, William's wife, gave birth to a boy, Herbert Geach, who was baptised in Trevethin Parish Church on 24th November 1831. He was Mary's first grandchild. She was forty-nine.

CHAPTER 5

1832-1836

From about 1832 onwards, John threw himself into politics full time. That year, there was a serious outbreak of cholera in the town. All the six wells were polluted and there was no efficient way to deal with sewage. The overcrowded slums in Friars Fields[24] had become a no-go area for respectable people. Lodging houses were filled to overflowing. Administratively, corruption and self-seeking reigned. There was no town hall, so meetings were held in one of the town's many public houses.[25]

For the next two years John was absorbed by local politics. His ultimate ambition was to be an MP. Mary ran the business. Presumably she had the help of a servant or shop assistant, as she had a growing family to care for. Young John was eighteen at the start of 1832 and had possibly already embarked on a career. At home with her still were Elizabeth, seventeen, and Sarah, nearly fifteen, who, if they were not continuing their education, could reasonably be expected to help. The four younger ones would certainly have been at school.

That year, too, her daughter, Mary Lawrence, gave birth to Mary's first granddaughter, another Mary. The family lived in Pontnewynydd and Mary Frost had her younger children and her duties in the shop, so although she would not have had very frequent contact with them, she would have been cheered by this event and glad that her eldest daughter was comfortably off. Through the

1830s, Mary Lawrence had at least five children: Mary, 1832, Elizabeth, 1833, John, 1835, Anne, 1837 and Henrietta in 1838. Her choice of names shows her closeness to the Frosts. She even feminised the name Henry making it Henrietta to name her youngest daughter. Her three elder children were baptised in the parish church at Trevethin but Anne's baptismal record shows they had moved to Raglan and George Lawrence is described as a gentleman. All of this meant contact with her mother was more difficult.

The Rev Jenkin Lewis had died in 1831 and had been replaced in Hope Chapel by Rev Benjamin Byron[26] who sympathised with the Frosts' radical views. At this time, many anti-slavery societies had been established throughout the country and Byron was a fervent abolitionist. A petition to Parliament for the abolition of slavery was sent from the 'Protestant Dissenters' of Hope Chapel, Newport.[27] This was a campaign the Frosts would have applauded. They were probably aware that earlier generations of the Morgans of Tredegar House had been investors in the Royal African Company, later the African Company of Merchants, a chartered monopoly that held exclusive rights to trade with West Africa and therefore to export enslaved humans to the Caribbean.[28] Women as well as men became politicised through the anti-slavery campaign, with the Rev Byron actively encouraging the participation of Newport women.

While Mary's life, of necessity, revolved around her family and the shop, John began to see a political road ahead. In September 1835, the Municipal Reform Act paved the way for John to become a town councillor later that year. This position gave him the power to fight for the rights of the poor and dispossessed. It also allowed him to open an investigation into the activities of his arch enemy, Thomas Prothero.

There were rumours suggesting their son John, disagreeing with his father's politics, could have emigrated to America at the end of 1835. There is a record of a John Frost, aged twenty-two, arriving in New York on 4th January 1836. It is known that some who emigrated to America changed their names to start afresh. If John did, it could explain why he cannot be traced and also why there is no record of his father and Catharine meeting him on their visit to the States in 1854. Certainly, young John Frost disappeared from the historical record. If he left the family, it must have been a great sadness for Mary. Another of her sons lost to her.

At the start of 1836, the newly constituted Newport town council met, and John Frost was a member. He wrote to the press constantly. In May, he took his oath to become a magistrate and became John Frost, Esquire. His status in the town and the good opinion of him held by many citizens would have reflected well upon Mary. He was constant in his efforts for the poor, and conscientious in his attendance at meetings. As a Poor Law Guardian, John had to attend meetings in Usk on Saturdays, the shop's busiest day. It brought great influence and prestige but more work for Mary. Working in a draper's shop could be strenuous as the rolls of heavy cloth had to be lifted from shelves to counters and back again. Shops at that time were open for very long hours, not closing until late in the evening.[29] Hard though it was for her, she ran the business as well as looking after her home and family, freeing up John. In this way, she made her contribution to the political struggle.

At least some of the family were able to take a holiday. In August 1836, William, his wife, little son Herbert and Miss Frost, presumably Elizabeth, were staying at a hotel in up and coming, fashionable, Llanwrtyd Wells.[30]

Elizabeth, then twenty-one years old, was clearly loved by her siblings and she appears over the years to be relied upon by them.

Growing up in a draper's shop in High Street would have had its advantages for the Frost girls, especially if they were interested in fashion. It surely made them the envy of their friends. They would have had their choice of the fabrics to sew their own clothes or take to a dressmaker. If the dressmaker on High Street, Mary Hopkins, did not suit them, then according to *Pigot's Trade Directory of 1835*, there were ten more dressmakers in the centre of Newport and a tailor rather fancifully named 'Taylor & Paradise'. There were also milliners, as no middle-class woman could go out without a bonnet. There was a staymaker. The high-waisted empire style of dress Mary would have worn in her youth had changed. Women's waists had returned to their natural position and tightly laced stays or corsets were worn to emphasise their slimness. There were shoemakers and on High Street too, a hairdresser's shop which sold perfume. In the Long Room on the first floor of the Custom House on Skinner Street, dancing lessons were available.[31] If such things did not interest them, I'm sure Napper's muffin and confectionary shop on their doorstep did not disappoint.

The wife of the wealthy Joseph Latch, mayor of Newport in 1835, shopped for some haberdashery requirements at Cambrian House where she ran up a bill that year for £16-9s-3d, (nearly £1,000 today) which would have been more than the annual wage of her lady's maid and, indeed, many of the other residents of Newport. She bought bonnets, hose, two to three pairs of shoes every month, dozens of yards of silk, velvet, bombazine, linen, crepe, muslin cambric, cotton, ribbon, chinchilla boas, pelisses and so on.[32] When, in November

1836, John became Mayor of Newport, it seems highly unlikely that Mary would attempt to emulate such extravagance. John was popular in the town, praised for his business-like efficiency and determined to use his advantages for the common good. Mary admired that.

When 1837 dawned, John was a town councillor, Justice of the Peace, an improvement commissioner, a guardian of the poor, a harbour commissioner and mayor of Newport. This, I think, must have been a high point in Mary's life, or perhaps a calm plateau. Her childbearing years were over. Her youngest child, Anne, was ten years old. The other girls were young ladies. Her Geach children were well married with their own growing families. Business was prospering, her husband respected and admired. The furniture sold to pay John's debts fifteen years ago had been replaced, not with the light, elegant furniture of the earlier Georgian era but with the heavier, substantial mahogany furniture favoured later in the century. Their home was comfortable and roomy enough for two pianos, one of them a grand![33] The dark days of John's imprisonment and their poverty were far behind. If she had a cause to be anxious, it was that John was upsetting the old enemy, the powerful and nasty Thomas Prothero. And he was an extremely dangerous adversary.

CHAPTER 6

1837-1838

If Mary was grieving the loss of their son, John, she also began to have serious concerns about her eldest son, William. She was becoming aware that he sailed close to the wind in at least some of his business dealings. He was a high-profile figure locally and often in the newspapers. In May 1837, Thomas Prothero and his colleague, Thomas Phillips, brought a case against him to stop him practising as a solicitor. He was accused of illegally signing an affidavit. It is evident that there was professional jealousy involved and the case was dismissed but William had to pay costs.

What would also have been abundantly clear to Mary was that Prothero was pursuing any avenue he could find to damage the Frost family and punish John for exposing the extortionate legal fees Prothero and Phillips charged their clients. Her son was providing them with opportunities to harm the family.

King William IV died in June 1837 and the Georgian era was over. As mayor, John had to proclaim the new Queen, eighteen-year-old Victoria.[34] There was little in the way of celebration in the town, unlike the previous coronation. And this was one of his last ceremonial duties before Prothero and Phillips blocked his re-election as mayor. They extracted their revenge for his constant exposing of their underhand dealings. But more retaliation was to come, and perhaps it was as well Mary did not know then how much more.

John began to spend more time in his study reading and writing. One day Mary came to him in tears because 'a very near relative had got into trouble of a most serious kind'.[35] In July 1838, William appeared before Newport magistrates, accused by Prothero and Phillips of forgery. It was again generally felt that this action was to damage John who, with Mary, supported William. However, the magistrates decided there was no evidence and William had a hero's welcome on returning home to Pontypool.[36] He decided to diversify his business and started importing timber, wheat and corn. Disturbing questions, however, were circulating about William's character.

Worries about William were put to the backs of their minds that summer as excitement grew amongst their radical friends. The London Working Men's Association had published a People's Charter. It had six points which demanded universal male suffrage, the removal of the property qualification for MPs, annual elections, equal constituency sizes, payment for MPs and secret ballots in elections. This was the catalyst. Chartism had arrived. It wanted to end the injustice of upper-class men formulating laws to their own advantage. The people's grievances were both their economic deprivation and their political oppression. Chartism aimed to solve both and it gave a focus to men and women's hopes and aspirations. Spreading the word and collecting signatures to petition for the Charter began. From this point on, Mary's life was to be changed forever by Chartism.

In the summer of 1838, the Working Men's Association of Newport was founded by William Edwards, a baker with a shop in Newport. The secretary of the Association was Samuel Etheridge, John's printer friend, who lived on High Street. William Anselm Townsend, aged twenty-three, was a very committed member and sometime treasurer. A one-time apprentice and foreman to Samuel Etheridge was John Partridge, who also printed many of the Chartist pamphlets. John Dickenson was a pork butcher with a shop on Commercial Street. He became one of the movement's leaders in Monmouthshire, doing a great deal of organising and speaking. They were all family men, and their mothers, sisters, wives and daughters were almost inevitably caught up in the excitement of this growing movement.[37] We do not know if Mary's friend, Ann Chiswell, and her husband, Henry, a butcher, were also part of this growing network. In the same house on Market Street lived Edward Frost, John's uncle, who was treasurer of the Newport Working Men's Association, so it is more than likely the Chiswells were involved, too.

John joined at the end of October when he was asked to convene a meeting and explain the Charter. At this meeting of about four to five hundred people, John announced his support for the Charter and became one of the leaders of the Monmouthshire Chartists. He explained the Charter in the Great Room in the Parrot Inn on the corner of Charles Street and Commercial Street. In his speech, which covered areas such natural rights and manhood suffrage, he stated that women were excluded by the order of nature and, rather disingenuously, that they already had power:

And other objection is made - why exclude women? This appears to be a natural exclusion. Providence has assigned to men and women distinct and different duties to perform; the duty of men is to attend to the more important affairs of life; that of women to domestic concerns. Men are called on to defend their country, to fight her battles at home and abroad, while women are not required to act, either as soldiers or as sailors. Indeed he thought that women had power enough already, and all present who were married would, no doubt, agree with him; for his own part he would no more think of acting in opposition to the advice of his wife, than he would think of burning his fingers over the candle; surely then it would be absurd to endeavour to give more power to the women, when already they are in possession of all.[38]

There seems little doubt Mary's views matched his and that her advice was acted on. It was power of a second-hand kind which, as a dutiful wife, she accepted, publicly at least.

Even if, as has been suggested, their son John had not agreed with his parents' political views, then they must have been gratified that their younger son, Henry, was enthusiastically involved. Along with other young men in Newport, many from the prominent Chartist families, he was a member of the youth wing of the Chartist movement. During his examination by magistrates in November 1839, his membership card was produced, showing he had been the very first member of the Newport Youths Democratic Association on 4th June 1839.

CHAPTER 7

1838-1839

In 1838 someone new came into the lives of the Frost family. A young man, Henry Vincent, was given responsibility by the London Working Men's Association for promoting universal suffrage and for forming Working Men's Associations in industrial South Wales and the West Country of England. He travelled the area, lecturing, forming societies, explaining and encouraging the signing of the Charter. Signatures were added to a petition which was to be presented to Parliament demanding the six points of the Charter be enacted.

He was a Chartist leader who unequivocally advocated votes for women. He was a ladies' man in every sense of the word. They adored him and he obviously revelled in their admiration. He was young, handsome and engaging. His visits to Newport throughout the spring of 1839, set many female hearts fluttering. The Frost girls must have been greatly envied when, because of his friendship with John, he was in their house. He considered that the setting up of Female Patriotic Associations were essential to Chartism's success[39] and the women in the town enthusiastically endorsed Newport's Female Patriotic Association. Vincent was addressed as 'brother' and he called women 'sisters' and was the only Chartist leader to convene women-only gatherings.[40]

MARY FROST

It was a time when people went regularly to church, or in the case of most of the Chartists, chapel. Non-conformity was an important factor in Chartism in Wales. The Frost family in Hope Chapel listened to long sermons, sang hymns, strove to become better, more caring people.

The social life of the chapel, with its events and meetings with like-minded friends, would also have been significant. It would probably not be too much to say that, for Mary and many women, this was the centre of their social circle. Nonconformist chapels offered new roles that women eagerly entered. They taught in the Sunday school, visited the poor and sick, distributed tracts, engaged in fundraising, supported missionaries, led class meetings, prayed with other women, and a few could preach to mixed audiences.

In a way, Chartism echoed this, with its meetings, lectures, ideas for improving their lives and their society. Women would have enjoyed the contact with their Chartist friends, the making of flags and banners, the intellectual stimulation and the excitement of the rallies which were like carnivals. These were whole family events including men, women and children. However, the visibility of women in Protestant sects was not mirrored in mainstream Chartist thinking which asserted that a woman's place was within the home and her main concern should be for her husband and family. Mary, early taught to believe herself second class, would not have found this as difficult to accept as maybe women of a later generation.

It is sad to say that all we know of individual Chartist women in Newport comes to us through the writings of men. The names of women were not often recorded. It would be good to think that this was to protect them, and that might be true in some cases. But women generally have a much lower profile in the historical record. They and their contributions were not considered to be worth noting. We therefore know the names of very few women Chartists and the ones we are aware of are known because of their family connections with male Chartists.

Yet these are the tip of the iceberg. At its height, the Newport Female Patriotic Society had hundreds of members. Mary and at least some of her daughters were members. John's mother, Sarah Roberts, too, was sympathetic and allowed a Chartist lodge to meet at the Royal Oak. There were many Chartist families living near the Frosts with active women members. The officers of the Newport Working Men's Association were regularly changed, and perhaps the women's organisation, too, provided opportunities for women to take on different responsibilities.

One Chartist family was that of William and Margaret Townsend. Their son William Anselm Townsend who was born in 1815 was an enthusiastic Chartist. There were also six daughters. We know that Sarah Frost was friends with one of them, Elizabeth Townsend. Quite probably there were friendships between the other Townsend and Frost girls, and they attended meetings and rallies together.

In 1839, Samuel Etheridge was a widower living with his daughter Martha who was then twenty-seven years old and ran a beer house in Caerleon. Samuel was a close associate of John and living so near each other, it is highly probable Martha Etheridge was also caught up in the Chartist movement. His former assistant John Partridge and his wife Leah had two sons and five daughters. One of their daughters, seventeen-year-old Amelia Partridge, was to play her own special part in this story.

MARY FROST

Another family who had a daughter we know was actively involved was the Dickenson family. John and Sarah Dickenson's daughter, Jane, about eighteen in 1839, was confident and articulate, chairing women's meetings and leading processions. Vincent described her as the 'presidentess', an awkward word indicating the difficulty he had in describing her role. She was a very unconventional young woman. She was a talented musician who used her ability in the service of Chartism as she played the piano at entertainments and fundraising concerts.

William Edwards became almost a full-time Chartist missionary, visiting the coalfields of Monmouthshire collecting signatures, speaking and recruiting. He was a baker, but he also sold Chartist papers. His wife, Sarah and sister, Mary Brewer,[41] were just as fervent and, in his absence, continued to sell radical literature. Mary Brewer collected signatures on the petition.

Slightly further afield in Malpas was Mary Simpson. Her husband was a gardener and they had two small children. They were Chartists and we know Mary Brewer was with them in their cottage on the day of the Rising, 4th November 1839. Another Chartist there on that day was James Aust, also a gardener living on the Malpas Road, almost opposite Malpas Court. With his wife Elizabeth, they hid Chartist money and membership cards in their cottage.

All these women, and many more, would have been known to the women in the Frost family, the wives and daughters friendly with Mary and her daughters. Like Sarah Frost and Elizabeth Townsend, there were sure to have been other friendships. Many of the older women would have become politicised in the earlier anti-slavery movement. This, sadly undocumented, network of active women would have encouraged and supported one another. And they would have needed this support. It took a strong woman to resist the pressures to be 'respectable' and Chartist women were subjected to public ridicule and abuse. To be forceful was considered unfeminine so the middle-class women particularly trod a very tricky path.

There is plenty of social commentary to be found in the great English novels of the 19th century, but Benjamin Disraeli, who later became Prime Minister, is the only author who wrote about a Chartist woman. His novel *Sybil* or *The Two Nations* was published in 1845. It centres on a female Chartist and takes a long look at the appalling conditions in which the country's working class lived.

So, the women were there, they were committed, but what did they expect Chartism to do for them? Women, like Mary, her daughters and her mother-in-law, were contributors to the wealth of the nation and family by their roles as shopkeepers, keepers of beer houses and lodging houses, domestic servants, shop assistants, and so forth, as well as their work in the mines and other heavy industries. In Newport, according to *Pigot's Trade Directory of 1835*, over fifty businesses were owned by women including some unexpected ones. Elizabeth Aston ran an iron foundry, Ann Lewis was a coal dealer, Margaret Francis was a butcher and Elizabeth Hill a blacksmith, as well as all the female grocers, drapers, dressmakers, milliners and so on. Were they not entitled to representation too?

Some women used the young Queen as their example in arguing that they should have their place in the political process. Others argued the case for giving the vote just to spinsters and the widowed. However, the inclusion of votes for women in the first draft of the Charter was soon dropped.

One reason for this appears to be tactical, that it was felt that to get agreement to this demand from Parliament was so unlikely that it would jeopardise the whole project. Women were therefore aware from the start that universal suffrage was not universal at all as it did not include them.

There is no doubt that Chartist men in general never saw women as equals. Most Chartist men, including John, did nothing to alter the presumption of the superiority and the rights of men.[12] Chartism was patriarchal, and no woman was ever a leader in the movement. Female support was encouraged as long as it offered that support from a subordinate position.

And the women seem to have accepted this. They reflected the thinking of the age regarding the traditional role of wives and mothers. They, especially the women in industries, mines and factories, resented having to work and that their children had to work. These poorer women particularly wanted to restore their domestic role, even though women at home were dependent on husbands, which confirmed their subordination. It is doubtful that most women even thought it was possible that they could attain social, economic and political equality. They trusted that once their men had the vote and could represent them politically, their lives would be improved. If men were paid a proper wage, women would not have to work outside the home. There was a Chartist slogan: 'No women's work except in the hearth and the schoolroom.'

Most female Chartists therefore did not see their interests being opposed to that of their menfolk. They worked together for what was essentially a masculine cause. As Professor Malcolm Chase put it, 'Ostensibly, women activists accepted the patronising stance of their male counterparts.'[43] A politicised woman's aim was to obtain the vote for men. Family and community loyalties were more important than women's rights. There was a sense of grievance which unified different classes and genders, for instance around issues such as the introduction of workhouses for the poor which separated men, women and children, and around children having to work. Dickens' *Oliver Twist*, published in 1838, highlighted the plight of many poor and unprotected children. People were also angry at the injustice of the iniquitous 'Truck System' which restricted their right to spend their money as they wished. Goods could only be purchased at the employer's Truck Shop where prices were generally higher. This affected women more than men. Obtaining the vote for their menfolk, not themselves, was seen as the necessary first step in righting the wrongs they felt.

How then did they play their part and support the Chartist movement?

Much female support was given from within the home or the domestic sphere. Mary would have agreed to host John's Chartist friends, providing food, a bed and whatever else was needed. Without this willingness, John's life as a Chartist would have been more difficult. Keeping a business going and being willing to put up with a husband's frequent absences allowed Chartist leaders like John to travel widely to promote the cause. This was not always easy for women and their sacrifices made a significant contribution to the movement.

Women oversaw the family finances and shopping. Mary, like other women, carefully chose where she shopped to encourage Chartist shopkeepers. The Frost shop would have gained custom from fellow Chartists. Shops which did not support the Charter would have been boycotted. Shopping then had a political meaning and gave women power.

MARY FROST

From the family finances also, women made their contributions to collections for the families of imprisoned Chartists. Knowing their wives and children were being taken care of, lessened a Chartist's concerns while in prison. In one case, a fund was set up to support Vincent's mother when he was imprisoned. Mary herself was to be helped by collections made by women's associations. Women were also known to have visited Chartist prisoners.

Money was raised by making and selling handicrafts, for example, articles of needlework. In addition, they embroidered banners, flags, sashes and caps of liberty. Green seems to have been the colour of choice for Chartist needlework. Catering for the Chartist tea parties and gatherings, decorating the meeting rooms with flowers and banners, all allowed women to do their bit while not departing from their traditional roles.

The main reason Henry Vincent encouraged the participation of women was because he saw them as educators.[44] Again, this was a conventional female occupation both within the home and in the schoolroom. They were to teach the children the principles of Chartism. According to general Chartist principles, girls were to be educated for a domestic role and not in order to be intellectually self-sufficient.

So far, so unobjectionable in early Victorian society. Not many patriarchal feathers would have been ruffled by any of this for, after all, this is the old, familiar middle-class philosophy of two spheres. It fitted neatly with Mary's 18th century upbringing.

But women's support for Chartism did not end there. They formed and ran their own local associations where they were in charge and were able to organise meetings. The Newport Female Patriotic Society arranged tea parties to honour visitors such as Henry Vincent. Jane

Dickenson often took the chair. They encouraged support amongst their friends and acquaintances. Most middle-class women of that time were pianists. We know there were two pianos in the Frosts' home. But the most able or confident pianist was Jane Dickenson who played in recitals to raise money for Chartist causes.

Women helped to run the great demonstrations and rallies. They also went from house to house to garner support, collect money and signatures. Over a thousand Monmouthshire women signed a separate charter. This was a very significant contribution because the Chartists' main strength lay in their numbers and the inclusion of women aided that. Many individual women, like Mary Brewer in Newport, took on 'male' roles like collecting lodge subscriptions and selling radical newspapers when their menfolk were in prison. Chartist newspapers were read with interest by women, and they wrote articles anonymously.

Women took to the streets, marching in processions. Protesting women gained more publicity and were considered more shocking than male protesters. For this, they were abused in the press. Women stepping outside their 'sphere' highlighted another dangerous aspect of Chartism for the ruling class. Politicised women demonstrating in the streets were an added threat to the powers that be. After the Newport Rising, women were blamed by the authorities for encouraging the men, which is perhaps a compliment to their enthusiasm and their influence.[45]

The traditional, predominately male, history of Chartism in Newport therefore is not the whole picture and never was. Women, like those in the Frost family, and many, many more, were there throughout, and although most names have been lost and lives forgotten, this book is an attempt to view those momentous times from a different point of view and to acknowledge the part played by Newport women in the Chartist movement.

The politicisation of women through their involvement with Chartism would have been empowering. Did they in subsequent decades view their traditional, female roles differently? Were they thereafter more inclined to question the status quo? For Mary and her daughters, these matters were to become even more complicated by the impact of the Newport Rising on their personal lives.

Sadly, despite the success of the women's groups, there was never an overarching national women's organisation as there was for men. The national Chartist movement organised a National Convention in London in early 1839 to make the arrangements for the presentation of the first petition. Delegates used the term MC, Member of Convention, to identify themselves. It was seen as an alternative parliament. Needless to say, not one of the delegates was a woman.

CHAPTER 8

1839 January to June

New Year's Day 1839 saw the first mass rally of Chartists in Monmouthshire. It was held at Pontnewynydd. It is said seven thousand people marched in procession with their banners. This huge gathering included men, women and children, full of optimism. John and Henry Vincent made speeches. Many of the Newport Chartists would have been there and probably some of John's family too. There was much excitement for it had a holiday atmosphere. People were urged to sign the charter and John was elected as delegate to the National Chartist Convention which placed him amongst the foremost Chartists in Britain. Going home that night the Frost family would have felt the added prestige. These were heady times.

On 4th February John was in London for the opening meeting of the Convention. Mary was used to coping on her own by this time and would have been glad he was playing such an important part in such a promising and worthwhile cause. They had high hopes for the success of this 'People's Parliament'.

Henry Vincent, meanwhile, had a major project in hand. On 23rd February 1839, the first issue of the *Western Vindicator* was edited, printed and published by him. He organised its distribution in South Wales and the West of England. The aim of the newspaper was to explain and to 'vindicate' the principles contained in the

People's Charter. In the first edition, Henry Vincent asked the question, 'What have women to do with politics?' and he himself gives the answer, 'All – everything!' In the first edition, too, was an address *To the Men and Women of the west of England and South Wales* in which he called for political equality. Each copy was eagerly looked forward to. John wrote many articles, especially early on. Women, too, wrote for the paper, although usually anonymously, using it to communicate with Vincent and other Chartists.

The paper was published weekly for ten months, documenting Vincent's missionary travels, Chartist meetings and individual Chartists, men and women. Without the accounts in the *Western Vindicator,* we would know of even fewer Chartist women and activities. He made a point of mentioning that ladies were present at his meetings and estimated their number. For instance, the report of the meeting in Newport on the evening of 19th March states a huge crowd of both men and women, in excess of three thousand, gathered out of doors to hear him speak.[46] All his addresses finished with three cheers for their sweethearts, wives and themselves.

On 20th March John missed what was probably a very important occasion for Mary, if not for him, for it was the wedding day of Sarah, the first of their daughters to be married. The family were committed members of Hope Chapel and Sarah had been baptised there. This building had been registered for solemnising marriages in 1837,[47] yet Sarah chose an Anglican Church, St Woolos, where the vicar who conducted the service, Rev A A Isaacson, was a Conservative and anti-Chartist.[48] Traditionally a bride's father paid for the wedding and gave the bride away. Whether John paid is not known but he certainly did not give the bride away as he was in London on

Chartist-related business on that day.[49] The only one of the Frost family who was definitely at the ceremony was her sister Ellen, aged eighteen, who acted as a witness. Was Mary there? She can hardly have greeted Sarah's choice of husband with delight.

Sarah married Harry Fry, a surgeon, aged thirty-three, from Somerset, who was over ten years her senior. It is recorded that he had been a military surgeon in the 14th Dragoons.[50] The London Provincial Medical Directories of 1850 and 1855 state he had been awarded a qualification in surgery in 1827 from the highly respected Imperial Academy of Surgery St Petersburg.

Were these claims credible? Harry Fry was not an honourable man. In 1826, he had been in court for seducing another man's wife and ordered to pay £2,000 (£135,000 today) to the wronged husband.[51] He had been imprisoned in Ilchester Gaol in 1831 for 'fraudulently claiming a certificate to practise as an apothecary'.[52] He was in court again early in 1836 for insolvency.[53] Was all this known to the Frost family? From 1836, he had been practising as a surgeon in Newport and applying, unsuccessfully, for the position of surgeon to the Board of Guardians.[54] The Frosts would have known he was an active anti-Chartist.

An announcement of their marriage was placed in the *Bristol Mercury* on Saturday, 23rd March and in the *Bristol Times and Mirror* of 30th March in addition to the Welsh papers.[55]

> *March 20 at St Woolos, Newport, Harry Fry, Esq., surgeon, to Sarah, second daughter of John Frost, Esq., one of H M Justices of the Peace for the County of Monmouthshire.*

Sarah must have realised what hurt this choice of husband would have been to her parents. She had grown up in a radical household and seen what sacrifices her parents had made for the Chartist cause, yet she threw her lot in with an out-spoken anti-Chartist. And a disreputable one at that. What a topic for the gossips in the town! All Mary's friends would have wondered and sympathised. In the parlance of the day, she had married to 'disoblige' her family. This was an obvious act of rebellion against her parents and all they stood for. It was not to be Sarah's last. For Mary, it was another of her children rejecting their fervent political views. How many family arguments had there been leading up to this? A rebellious daughter is not conducive to harmony in any home and the other children would have been listeners, if not participants, in any disagreements. Despite this, John always considered his home a happy place[56] which is perhaps a great tribute to Mary's management and diplomacy.

On the same day, there was a huge Chartist women's gathering held at the Bush Inn in Newport. It was chaired by Jane Dickenson, and Vincent was again present.[57] Five days later, Vincent returned to Newport for a tea party arranged by the Chartist women. It was attended by hundreds. The later evening meeting ended with a procession through the town. They proceeded four abreast with the women first, perhaps because the authorities were less likely to break up a line of women and so in this way, they protected the men. As they passed the Frost's house, they gave three cheers for Mary, who was clearly popular.[58] She was not on the streets with them, however, and we do not know whether any of her daughters were. Jane Dickenson's is the only name in the account. Vincent's comments on that day in the *Western Vindicator* of 4th April were, 'The Newport ladies are progressing with great spirit to the terror of the Aristocrats of the town and neighbourhood'. Two days later, he was with then again and addressed an evening meeting for the women. So many wanted to attend that a larger room had to be found. Again, it was chaired by Jane Dickenson. All these women, caught up in the exhilaration, would have added to the tension building up in the town.

The *Monmouthshire Merlin*, an anti-Chartist paper, reported on 20th April on Vincent's meeting at the Bush Inn which terminated at 8p.m. with a procession along Commercial Street to Pentonville. 'The rear of the column was brought up by some draggle-tail females, denizens of the Paphian bowers of Mill Street and Friars Fields, who fully participated in the wild fanaticism of their male coadjutors.'[59] Another procession in High Street was 'preceded by a great rout of boys and idle women…' In another edition it stated, 'The Female Political Union is sure to cleanse the national impurities, being always headed by a chair woman.'[60]

Throughout this period, John split his time between the Convention and travelling the country, speaking to as many people as he could.[61] He was home from time to time but Mary must have been well used to his comings and goings. Vincent, too, exhausted himself with his non-stop travels and constant speaking engagements. For the Frost household, the tension and excitement must have been palpable. They believed things were going the Chartists' way and the authorities were plainly rattled. For Mary, there was the added dimension that the people condemning the Chartists were the type of people she grew up and mixed with until she met John. Their views were known to her personally.

It is difficult these days to comprehend the fear that the upper classes and nouveau rich industrialists had of violent revolution by the working classes in the early 19th century. Shock at the French Revolution in 1789 was still felt. It was really believed that violence would erupt in Newport. Defensive structures were built for protection. One example is the wall which was constructed round The Mynde (now 14 High Street) in Caerleon in 1839. The owner of the house, and of Ponthir Plate Works, John Jenkins, was frightened by the possibility of violence and destruction by the Chartists and built the wall right round his property to protect it. On 12th April, Sarah's husband, Harry Fry, attended an anti-Chartist meeting in Christchurch. At this meeting also were Thomas Prothero, Thomas Phillips and the town clerk, Thomas Jones Phillips, all adversaries of the Frost family. There were plans to form a local militia. Harry Fry seconded a resolution proposed by Thomas Jones Phillips thanking the chairman. His openly anti-Chartist stance and alignment with the men John and Mary despised must have caused hurt and embarrassment to his parents-in-law.

Henry Vincent spoke to the crowds on 25th April from a window in the Frosts' house. Government spies were by now following Vincent, seeking evidence to arrest and convict him at a time when transportation to Australia or death by hanging were some of the punishments for stirring up social unrest. It was brave of Mary to allow a marked man like Vincent into her home but then her husband was being spied on too, and Mary was at least as committed to the cause as them. The crowd moved away from the Frost house at the urging of William Anselm Townsend and held a further gathering at Rodney Parade.[62] The women's meeting two days later needed a large room as so many wanted to be involved. The proceedings started at 10 o'clock and finished at midnight!

As spring turned to summer, there was no let-up to the tension in Newport. On 2nd May, a company of the

29th Regiment arrived at Newport and others were billeted at Abergavenny and Monmouth. John believed many of the soldiers being drafted into the area were Chartist sympathisers so would not move against them. If Mary believed him, it must have consoled her a little, but as a mother of daughters, she would have been apprehensive about the number of unknown single men on the streets of the town.

A Royal Proclamation was signed on 3rd May, empowering magistrates to outlaw any Chartist meeting at will. The Newport anti-Chartists were ready and when, on Tuesday 7th May, Home Secretary John Russell circulated a printed document to magistrates telling them to take the necessary measures for the suppression of illegal meetings, they acted.

On that day, William Edwards, John Dickenson and William Anselm Townsend were arrested. The prisoners were held initially in the King's Head Hotel in High Street. Feelings were running high in the town. On the street outside, women, some with children, gathered to protest. Things became heated and the police started taking the protesters into custody. One woman pelted a special constable with stones and got herself arrested.[63]

John, who had just returned from London, appealed for calm from the upstairs window of a building opposite the King's Head while he negotiated with the magistrates for the release of the arrested protesters, then he successfully urged the crowd to go home. There was concern he would be arrested, too, increasing Mary's anxiety.

Vincent was arrested in London. Two days later, he appeared with Edwards, Dickenson and Townsend before Newport Magistrates at the King's Head Hotel. The women were devastated. The four prisoners, handcuffed, were put in a wagon to be taken to Monmouth Gaol, and women as well as men attempted to free them but were beaten back. The heavy-handed treatment of the protesters gave them further reason to become antagonistic. Although the arrests were always on the cards, the reality of having their friends and colleagues taken into custody was sobering.

Without doubt, the Frost family would have supported the womenfolk of the arrested men: John Dickenson's wife Sarah and daughter Jane; William Edwards' wife Sarah and sister Mary Brewer; William Anselm Townsend's mother, Margaret, and his sisters. Mary particularly could remember her own feelings when John was arrested and imprisoned sixteen years previously. All these families were well known as they had shops in the centre of Newport and there was much sympathy for them throughout the town. The Chartists' call, 'Keep the Peace', was changing to the more ambiguous, 'Peacefully if we may. Forcibly if we must.'[64]

The *Western Vindicator* of 18th May printed Vincent's first letter from prison on its front page. He included the following greeting: 'And above all let our lovely and patriotic females smile upon us all - back us with their sympathy - and uphold us with their prayers.' Some of the Newport women then asked him if they could visit him in prison and he replied, again via the *Western Vindicator*, 'Yes, you can see us through our iron bars; and we shall be very glad to see you, or any, or all of the Radical ladies of Newport. I assure you Monmouth gaol is a very clean mansion.'[65]

The Convention was adjourned so John would have returned home in time for the Whit Monday rally on 20th May. This was a huge family meeting, held in Blackwood. According to *The Charter* of 26th May, there were 30,000 people present. Speeches deplored the imprisonment and appalling treatment of Vincent, Dickenson, Edwards and Townsend, who should have had the privileged conditions of political prisoners.[66] Support for the Charter and the collection of signatures were urged, against a carnival atmosphere with music, flags, singing. This is an example of a Chartist song which was printed in the *Western Vindicator* on 21st September 1839. Disappointingly despite its title, after the first two lines, it addresses men and emphasises women's decorative and supportive role.

TO THE FEMALE DEMOCRATS

Hail! sisters, whose motives are noble and glorious;
Long sacred your names, to fair freedom shall be;
Hurrah for the cause, for it must be victorious,
The women are with us, and we shall be free.

Where's he that would shrink in the moment of danger?
Where's he that refuses our labour to share?
Who looks on our cause with the eye of a stranger,
When supported by justice, by truth, and the fair?

Arouse from your lethargy, children of slavery,
And join with the holy, the brotherly band;
Awake from the slumber of priestcraft and knavery,
And the demon "Oppression," will fly from the land.

Then then, shall we welcome the bright sun freedom;
No fetters of tyrants our children shall wear;
To democracy onward our sisters will lead them,
And they shall be free as their mothers are fair.

SONGS FOR THE PEOPLE

MARY FROST

The excitement of the event would have been tempered for Mary by another blow: the distressing news that William had been declared bankrupt. Many of his extravagant possessions and household effects were auctioned. As an indication of William's lifestyle, these are some of the items which were listed in the *Monmouthshire Beacon* on 29th June: elegant and modern furniture, foreign and English china, richly cut glass, 500 ounces of plate, valuable paintings and engravings, thirty dozen bottles of choice wine, a phaeton, a gig, a horse, a pony and a Newfoundland dog. Quite possibly he had moved back to Bristol by this time, but it is doubtful whether his wife, Elizabeth, and their son, Herbert, went with him. They probably stayed in Pontypool near her family.

Throughout June, John toured the country, returning to Newport for a short while in July for a meeting of the town council. The family would have looked forward to the time he was at home, bringing news of other areas and other people. By now, Mary would have been used to running the business, but that, with the domestic duties and the Chartist activities, must have been exhausting. Mary was fifty-seven years old and losing the resilience of youth.

CHAPTER 9

July to October 1839

Everything that the Chartists had been working for, the petition with over 1.2 million signatures, was at last delivered to Parliament in a decorated cart on 12th July. So many hopes were pinned on it but it was rejected by a huge majority. The disappointment was immense. How could the Chartists now achieve their aims? The Frosts surely discussed their options.

On 15th July, the Female Patriotic Society of Newport wrote an open letter to Henry Vincent which was printed in the *Western Vindicator* on 27th July. In their letter, they begin by congratulating him on his release on bail. Most of the letter, however, is a criticism of the 'men in authority' in the town. They single out a 'petty local tyrant' with a 'virulent acidity of temper' whose recent actions 'added moral deformity to a physical frame naturally repulsive'. No mincing their words! Their admiration for Vincent produced a torrent of abuse aimed at his enemies. They sent him £2 (£120 today) towards his defence fund in addition to money already sent. The women's letter contains invective which equals that in John's letters and pamphlets. The 'tyrant' would have been incensed. In the same edition, John also has a long article including a section which ridicules the authorities for their fear of the ladies' tea meetings convened by the 'wives and daughters of the town'.

The trial of Vincent, Edwards, Townsend and Dickenson on 2nd August was another watershed moment in the events leading, it seemed almost inexorably, towards disaster. Vincent was sentenced to one year's imprisonment, William Edwards to nine months, John Dickenson and William Anselm Townsend to six months. Feelings were running high, as by Chartist standards these men were innocent.

Mary and other members of the Female Patriotic Society of Newport would have continued their support for the families of these men but it is interesting that, after her father's imprisonment, we do not hear any more about Jane Dickenson. She continued to support Chartism as later events showed, but perhaps there was a concern that she, too, could be targeted by the authorities. Sarah, John Dickenson's wife, visited the prisoners but whether she took her daughter with her is not noted.

John continued to urge calm although he also felt personally in danger of the authorities and Mary and the family were on edge. There was a Chartist service at Hope Chapel, the minister, Benjamin Byron, being a supporter. Two hundred people attended. There was also an enormous demonstration at Dukestown, Tredegar.[67] This gathering, one of the largest in the entire 19th century, consisted of about 40,000 supporters.[68] The excitement must have been enormous. John, the principal speaker, took their son Henry Hunt. The Frost women are not mentioned but it is highly probable they were there, too. The increasing involvement of Henry, then aged seventeen, in his father's Chartist activities, is another indication of the strength of Mary's commitment. It appears Henry was being used as a messenger across the area.

Mary probably saw little of John in September as he was travelling the country, speaking at meetings. But, to her relief, he remained free unlike Vincent, Edwards, Dickenson and Townsend. She would have been horrified to hear that when Sarah Edwards went to Monmouth Gaol to see her husband, William, she was refused admission.[69] On 7th September, young William Anselm Townsend was moved from Monmouth Gaol to Milbank Penitentiary in London, another blow to his family.[70] John wrote many letters to the authorities, arguing for better treatment of the prisoners.[71] He could call upon his own treatment at Cold Bath Fields. Mary, too, would remember the feelings of having a husband ill-treated in prison.

The last of the big Chartist rallies was held on 3rd October at the Royal Oak, Coalbrookvale, owned by Zephaniah Williams. Five hundred men, riotous, wanted to free Vincent and his fellow prisoners. John persuaded them to be calm and patient, telling them he was going to stand for Parliament at the election he saw coming soon and would press their case. He was trying very hard to keep a lid on things. John knew that spies, double agents and agents provocateurs were joining the movement. He must have been aware that he could no longer restrain the Welsh Chartists who were determined on action. This tension was affecting his health which was an added worry for Mary. He was home in Newport and the surrounding areas for most of October but he was unwell and spent the final fortnight confined to his bed.

CHAPTER 10

November 1839

When John left for Blackwood,[72] early on Friday, 1st November, how could Mary have known that John would never return to their home in Newport again? She knew things were coming to a head, she knew something momentous was going to happen, but did she continue to think John could contain it? Maybe she believed that a huge show of strength was planned to protest at the treatment of Vincent and the other prisoners. Her mind would have been fluctuating around the possible outcomes. Could John continue to pacify those who wanted more than a peaceful demonstration? Had it already got beyond that? A demonstration of strength could easily get out of hand, especially, as she well knew, some men were preparing to carry weapons.

Newport was home to John's bitterest enemies whom he had been unable to defeat by lawful means. Could he resist the opportunity to strike at Newport's corrupt seat of power? Did she fear that that old impulsive desire of John's to attack his enemies would have its opportunity? Did she know that part of the plan was to kidnap Thomas Prothero at Malpas Court on the way to Newport? But alongside this, she knew John was not the sort of man who could lead a battle. All of this must have been swirling round in Mary's mind. John was convinced that most of the citizens of Newport were sympathetic to Chartism and he also believed that the soldiers would not attack civilians. Perhaps, like John, she felt events had to take their course. If the details were not worked out until that weekend in Blackwood, then she would not have known what to expect. Her daughters would have been even less in the picture. What Mary knew, only after John had left, was that, over that weekend, the authorities were rounding up the Newport Chartists and holding them. In addition, hundreds of special constables were being enrolled to defend the town.

An active member of one of the Blackwood Chartist lodges, which held its meetings at the Coach and Horses, twenty-one-year-old William Davies, was well known to the Frost family.[73] His father, Roger, had known John for about twenty years and he kept a successful shop in Blackwood which, along with his wife's inheritance, meant they lived a comfortable middle-class life. Like the Frosts, they were non-conformists. William was well educated and destined to continue his father's business. He became an enthusiastic Chartist, was close to John and was used by him as a trusted messenger and go-between. He was to become a particular friend of Ellen Frost.

On Saturday 2nd November, William Davies[74] visited Newport and called at the Frost's house. Mary asked him to carry letters to John which suggests the Frost's house was some sort of centre for Chartist messaging. While John was away, Mary sent letters and parcels to John by any messenger she could, and she would have been fully aware of the dangers. That Saturday and Sunday, John stayed in Blackwood. In Newport, the contingents of newly sworn in special constables patrolled the streets, increasing the tension. The leading Chartists were held in the Westgate Hotel and in the Workhouse on Stow Hill. Mary and the whole of Newport was on edge.

MARY FROST

At daybreak on Monday 4th November, the mayor, Thomas Phillips, was ready. The authorities were in no doubt the time had come. The Chartists, thousands of them, armed and determined, had marched in torrential rain throughout the night down the valleys leading to Newport, along roads, such as they were, running in water. John led them, splashing and noisy, down Stow Hill. The women waited horrified, frightened, excited. Anything was possible.

The men arrived at the Westgate Hotel by about nine-thirty. For about twenty-five minutes, there were the sounds of windows smashing, then guns firing. All of this commotion must have been heard by Mary and the family. It seems incredible that John led thousands of armed men to within a few hundred yards of his wife and daughters. There was panic and confusion. Death, injuries, rumours. Where was John?

He was seen in Tredegar Park later in the morning, apparently terribly upset. Did anyone tell the Frost family? Henry, too, was out and about, increasing Mary's anxiety. Dozens of wounded men who had not been able to get away were being taken to the homes of Chartists.[75] Were any of the injured men bandaged and fed by the Frost women and helped to get home? Everyone's story was different, but one thing was indisputable: the Rising had failed.

Mary Brewer had been in the Malpas home of fellow Chartist Mary Simpson that morning, waiting for news. She later ventured into Newport for information. She would have seen the dead and dying who were still lying in Westgate Square. Did she call on the Frosts?

Thomas Phillips, the mayor, had been injured in the exchange of shots at the Westgate. His mentor and colleague, Thomas Prothero, was not around as he and his family had left Newport for safety elsewhere. Thomas

Jones Phillips, clerk to the magistrates, led the investigation. He wanted to capture the Chartists who had run from the Westgate battle and he wanted evidence for the trials. He interviewed shopkeepers, inn keepers and other witnesses. Large rewards were offered. Bills were posted offering £100 reward (£6,000 today) for the capture of John and his fellow leaders.

Late in the afternoon, he arrived at the Frosts' home in High Street demanding John's papers. A servant opened the door to the group of men and took them into the room where Mary and her daughters were waiting, hearts beating, no doubt. November evenings are cold and dark. There would be a fire in the grate and smoky oil lamps or flickering candles. The family sitting, devastated. The women allowed Phillips' men to go to John's study at the back of the house.[76] What choice did they have? Two of Mary's daughters went with them - which two, Elizabeth and Catharine?

In this account, Elizabeth has emerged as the reliable daughter, the one who supported family members, the one who could take her mother's place, if need be. It was not Mary, so it was probably Elizabeth who took up the task of handing over John's papers. Perhaps Mary, usually so strong, committed and resourceful, let her daughters take control. Perhaps she could not bring herself to co-operate with the enemy. Elizabeth, from her earliest days, would have been used to seeing her father sitting in his study among his papers, reading and writing. She trusted that night that he would not have left anything incriminating, for she probably knew that Chartists' papers had been hurriedly burned in households all over the area, both immediately before and after the Rising.[77] In his study would have been his notes, drafts of articles, pamphlets and letters. She carefully bundled them and handed them over. As the officers took a large quantity of John's private papers, it was as if a part of her father was being taken away. The space the papers left would be a constant reminder of the space in the home John was leaving. What Mary and the family could not have known, in their concern, was that John was only a stone's throw away, trying to make his way home without detection.

Phillips' men, armed special constables led by Stephen Rogers, continued their search of Newport. It went on throughout the evening, arrest after arrest. At about seven o'clock, they arrived at the home of John Partridge to confiscate his papers. They knocked.

The members of the family of the Chartist printer John Partridge were also friends of the Frosts. Their home was positioned to the back of the Frost house and could be reached by a passage through the garden into Pentonville, the area to the north behind High Street.[78] It was the Partridge house where John and fellow Chartist, Charles Waters, had arrived secretly that evening, tired, wet, hungry, miserable, intent on getting home unnoticed. John wanted to say goodbye to his family before going into hiding.[79] He borrowed some of Partridge's clothes as his sailor coat and red cravat were soaked.[80]

In the house was Amelia, aged seventeen, looking after her father and her five-year-old brother. After she had put her little brother to bed, she was sent out by John to buy cheese and beer, armed with a shilling from John. This is strange. Is it likely the Partridge family were living hand-to-mouth to the extent that they had no food in the house to give John? It seems to me the men wanted Amelia out of earshot for a while. While she was out, did she call into the Frost house to tell them John was safe? This could well be what John was hoping as he sent her out to the shops. She obviously knew the Frost family as she was of an age with the Frost daughters. Also, in later statements under official questioning, she said the Frost house was better and more comfortable than hers, making clear she had at some time been a visitor there. It is more than likely both families were accustomed to meet too at Chartist rallies and meetings. But in Newport this was no ordinary evening. Bodies were still lying in the street outside the Westgate Hotel, abandoned weapons strewn around, soldiers kept guard and the police and town officials were going to the homes of all known Chartists, seizing papers and other evidence. There was a price on her father's head and John's too. She was an intelligent girl so perhaps she did John's shopping quickly and returned home.

In Amelia's evidence to the magistrates, she stated that, after giving John his cheese and beer, she went out again to see her friend Ann Lewis.[81] Again, was she encouraged to leave? Did her father feel she would be safer with her friend? Ann Lewis was eighteen and living at home with her parents in Pentonville. Amelia admitted seeing Mrs Chiswell, Mary's friend, although she denied knowing she was Mary's friend and said she did not mention John. As the magistrates remarked, she was a bright girl, doubtless she would not admit to this, whatever the truth of the matter. One cannot imagine that she would not have passed this news on to Mary's friend, especially as she had already told Ann Lewis. The probability is, therefore, that by this time, Mary knew where John was.

Phillips and his men knocked on the Partridge door, intent on confiscating any incriminating papers, and then broke in. To their absolute surprise, they found John eating his cheese. He, Waters and Partridge were promptly arrested and, once an escort had arrived, were marched away. John begged to be allowed to go into his own house as he passed it. His clothes and shoes were still wet, and he said he needed to change but he was refused. One of the officers stated that John gave Phillips his watch and chain and £20 (£1,200 today) in gold to give to Mary 'for their use'.[82]

By this point, someone, if not Amelia, must have informed Mary. It is also entirely possible that, hearing the breaking down of the Partridge's door and the arrest of the men, they were at their window or in the street watching when John and his fellow prisoners passed their house on the way to the Westgate. At least they knew he was alive. But they also knew that the Rising had been a disaster. They were not the only family in Newport that night who were left without their menfolk. I suspect there was little sleep.

Thomas Prothero returned to Newport to lead the inquisition. He threw himself into the questioning of the accused. How delighted he must have been when, on Tuesday, John appeared before the magistrates in the Westgate Hotel, charged with high treason. Mary and her daughters went to the Westgate on Tuesday morning and to their relief, the magistrates allowed them to see and talk to John.[83] In a letter to Mary on Christmas Day, he wrote how much he appreciated seeing her face and those of Catharine and Ellen. Before daybreak on Wednesday, he and the other prisoners were taken by armed guard to Monmouth Gaol. Mary and the family, again, had to cope with John in prison. His future and theirs were very uncertain.

By Wednesday, shops were beginning to open again but for days after the uprising, the arrival of yet more troops made Newport appear like a garrison town, with soldiers with fixed bayonets on the streets. People flooded into Newport seeking news of marchers who had not returned home. Mary must have been horrified by the rumours and wild stories which gradually took the place of shock and relief amongst the townspeople. Tales were circulating that John's daughters were seen outside the Westgate on that fateful morning, waving handkerchiefs to encourage the Chartists. This was stoutly denied.[84]

Another rumour arose that, on Sunday 17th November, John's friend William Prowting Roberts, a Bath solicitor, went to Blackwood with two of Mary's daughters, disguised as servants.[85] Was this true? Presumably he was collecting evidence for the defence. Why was he accompanied by the two Frost women and which two were they? Perhaps they went because they knew more about their father's activities and friends in the area than Roberts. Was one of the two women Ellen Frost, hoping for news of William Davies who had not been with the marchers but had been seen leaving Blackwood on the 4th? If they were close friends, she could have known his family and associates better than the others and so been of more use to Roberts. The point of the disguises presumably was because, if Roberts were seen with members of the Frost family, his intentions would have been obvious. Roberts was arrested so the authorities certainly did have their eyes on him, but the two women were not arrested - probably to their relief and to Mary's. If the story were true, she must have been on tenterhooks all the time they were away. William Prowting Roberts was brought before the magistrates but was dismissed without charge. In another report, John's daughters visited a solicitor in Bristol to aid John's defence.[86]

The Chartist papers, of course, took a different line from the anti-Chartist mainstream press. The *Northern Liberator* sent a correspondent to Newport to talk to the Frost family. He described them as an interesting and amiable family and reported that they were displaying great fortitude and were in good spirits. On the evening he visited them, Mary was with her four daughters and the fifth, a married lady, obviously Sarah, was visiting. The following morning, he accompanied Miss Frost on a visit to Monmouth Gaol. She was allowed to see John for three quarters of an hour in the Governor's house. Afterwards, he reported, she was very upset and described her as 'the purest embodiment of filial affection'. The family so impressed him that he could understand why they were held in such high regard.[87]

It is at this point that William Foster Geach threw himself into the defence of his family. Henry Hunt Frost, his seventeen-year-old half-brother, was arrested, taken into custody without a warrant, and brought before the magistrates on 14th November. Mary must have been distraught. William mounted a spirited defence. Although Henry was discharged, because he was not carrying arms, it was rumoured that he was on the run for many months, the newspapers claiming he had absconded. William indignantly denied this. His efforts on behalf of his family must have been one ray of light in Mary's bleak existence. John wrote to William, asking him to visit him in prison. William felt 'duty bound, by ties of kindred' to help the family in any way he could, although financing a legal team for John was beyond his means.[88] However, he put time, effort and skill into organising John's defence and the support he gave to his mother and John during this time was enormous.

The authorities were still out rounding up suspects and witnesses, collecting as much evidence as possible. In order to obtain witnesses for the Crown, wives of some of the Chartists were induced to give evidence. In the town, feelings were split as many of the shopkeepers and professional people agreed to be witnesses for the prosecution. A midnight raid was made on the shop of Sarah Edwards who was selling Chartist newspapers while her husband was in prison. All her papers were seized, including copies of the *Northern Star* and the *Western Vindicator*. All known Chartists were being harassed. Each time a member of the Frost household went out, the topic of conversation with everyone they met would have been the Rising, the arrests and John's trial. The anxiety must have been intolerable.

Rev Benjamin Byron's house was searched to no effect and he continued to pray for John at every service, which would have given the family some consolation. Their friends and fellow Chartists were highly active on behalf of the prisoners. Meetings were held, including some ladies' tea parties. Funds were raised all over the country for their defence. Some of this was passed to William Foster Geach.[89] Did anyone question whether he was the wisest person to put in charge of this fund? With money pouring in for the prisoners' defence, two remarkable legal men were engaged for the defence: Fitzroy Kelly and Sir Frederick Pollock. William took on the gathering of the background information for them.

Throughout this time, Mary would have had to ask herself how responsible John was for the way things had gone so disastrously wrong on that fateful march. She still believed in the Chartist cause and all John stood for, believing he acted in good faith with the best of intentions. She would also have questioned whether she could or should have used her influence with him to prevent this tragedy. For such a conscientious woman, it was a time of great heart searching.

William Davies was discovered in Canterbury on 1st November at the home of an uncle, his father's brother. Where he had been since he had been seen leaving Blackwood on 4th November is unknown. Did Ellen know? He was planning to escape to France. He was returned to Newport and appeared before the magistrates in the Westgate on 5th December. He was charged with conspiracy and riot. This lesser charge was because, it appeared, he did not take part in the march but remained in Blackwood on the night of the 3rd/4th. At the Coach and Horses, John had told him to go home as he was unwell. Was John protecting him, knowing his daughter Ellen was fond of him? He was kept in custody for six days, then released on bail. His father, Roger, was trying to do what he thought best for his son and was continually active on his behalf, trying to extricate him.

CHAPTER 11

December 1839

Near the end of a tumultuous year, Mary's second grandson was born. On 12th December, Sarah gave birth and she decided to give her son the name Dennis Fitzroy Kelly Fry, the middle two names being those of the barrister who was to defend her father at his trial. It was a public show of loyalty to her family. Although Mary already had grandchildren by William and Mary Geach, Dennis was John's first grandchild. Did he ever see him?

If this birth brought Mary some much-needed cheer, it was short-lived, for the family then received a terrible blow: it was announced that Blackwood Chartist William Davies had turned Queen's Evidence and was going to testify for the prosecution in John's trial which was scheduled to begin on 31st December. A crucial witness, he was buying his own safety by incriminating John. This was a shattering betrayal. One cannot imagine the distress of Mary, Ellen and the other Frost women. Fearing the worst, John began the process to transfer ownership of the Royal Oak to his mother so that it could not be confiscated.

Mary visited John in Monmouth Gaol on Saturday 9th December, according to the *Monmouthshire Merlin*.[90] The *Champion and Weekly Herald*, a London paper, reported a visit by her the following Saturday, too, and it added, 'The poor lady bears her heavy affliction with surprising fortitude...' John was described as 'dejected' at the thought of his family, 'to all of whom he was ardently attached'.[91] Reading between the lines of this, it seems that Mary was determined to show her strength and support of John through this dreadful time. Her pride would not allow her to show her devastation openly.

A public thanksgiving was held in Newport on 18th December for the escape from the Chartist uprising, organised by the town authorities.[92] All shops, inns and alehouses were ordered to close and there were services in St Woolos Church and St Paul's. Needless to say, the relatives of the Frost family did not participate or close their premises. They were said to be 'careless of the consequences'.[93]

In the *Monmouthshire Merlin* on 21st December 1839, the following advertisement appeared, placed by Henry M Partridge, Auctioneer, of Commercial Street:

NEWPORT, MONMOUTHSHIRE.

TO BE SOLD BY AUCTION,

(WITHOUT THE LEAST RESERVE)

By Mr. H M PARTRIDGE

On SATURDAY and MONDAY, the 28th and 30th December 1839,

on the Premises in HIGH STREET,

All THE HOUSEHOLD FURNITURE,

And the Remaining Part of

THE STOCK-IN-TRADE, &c.,

OF MR. JOHN FROST.

THE HOUSEHOLD FURNITURE comprises Four Post, Tent and Stump Bedsteads, with dimity and moreen Furniture; several excellent Goose Feather Beds; Millpuff and Straw Mattresses; Mahogany Dining, Breakfast, Pembroke, and

Round Tables; Round and Square Deal do; Chimney and Pier Glasses, in gilt frames; Swing Dressing do., in mahogany frames; Mahogany and Painted, Dressing Tables, and Washstands; Square and Sweep Front Chests of Drawers; Mahogany Work Table, on pillar; Set of Three do.; large Square Sofa, with chintz cover; Loose Swabs and Pillows; Mahogany Frame Chairs, in hair seating; Green Window, and Fancy Bedroom do.; Bronzed, Wire and other Fenders; Sets of Fire Irons; Bedside and Room Carpets; Floor Cloth; Square Piano-forte; Grand do., in mahogany cases; Mahogany Butler's Tray; do. Knife Case; Japanned Trays and Waiters; Bed and Table Linen; China Glass and Earthenware; Kitchen Utensils, &c.

The STOCK includes a general assortment of Linen Drapery, Hosiery, &c., &c.

The Stock-in-Trade will be sold on Saturday, and the Household Furniture on Monday, and the Sale will commence on each day precisely at Eleven o'clock. The whole may be seen between the hours of Ten and Four on the Day preceding the Sale.

So, again, Mary was selling their furniture and the stock in the shop. Again, John needed the money, so she was tasked with breaking up their family home, each piece scrutinised and itemised by the auction house. She and the children were to spend Christmas with all their possessions around them and then, on the day after Boxing Day, their home was to be opened to prospective buyers inspecting the contents. Was this surplus furniture? Even though Victorian homes were usually overstuffed, this seems a great deal to be just surplus. Many of these items are large pieces of furniture and so the rooms must have been very spacious. And while this inventory is fascinating in the light it throws on their lives, it is also interesting to note what is not offered for sale. Where are the desks, especially John's, wardrobes, bookcases, paintings, bureaux or objets d'art? Mary is selling bedlinen and tablecloths but not curtains. Could friends be buying the Frosts' possessions and allowing them to continue to use them?

Or were the family planning on moving out? If so, where were they going? According to the *Morning Chronicle*, rumours were circulating that the Frost family were making arrangements to leave the country when John was acquitted.[94] In addition to the sale of her furniture, Mary sold an annuity and gave the money to the defence fund.

John wrote to Mary from Monmouth Gaol on Christmas Day:

> *My Dearest Mary,*
>
> *In the many trials and difficulties which we have met with during a period of twenty-seven years, you have discovered fortitude to bear affliction seldom exceeded by woman. Now, then, my love, is the time to call forth all you possess...*

He urged her not to look back and reflect on what might have been done differently but to face the worst that could happen. The performance of her duty to others would be weakened by grief. He recognised her anxiety and was concerned that whatever the verdict of the trial, a sudden shock would have serious consequences for her. He knew the death sentence was a real possibility but he believed in the immortality of the soul and urged her to draw strength from her faith. They would meet again in eternity. He asked that his son and daughters 'bear this great trial with calm resignation'.

On a more practical note, he advised her to stay in the same home and carry on with the business, if possible, to give his daughters employment. He also wished his 'poor old mother' to live with them. He was adamant that neither Mary nor any of the family should visit him.[95] With none of these practical requests did Mary comply. Nor did she need to be told she must find the strength to cope. She had coped before and she would again. This time her children were older and were a support to her.

At the end of the year, Mary was sent various amounts of money raised by Chartists throughout the country for John's defence. Some of the money raised had been from separate women's collections.[96] New Year's Eve 1839 saw the start of John's trial and the end of what must have been one of the worst years of Mary's life. The future was too painful to contemplate.

CHAPTER 12

1840 January to June

At the start of the 1840s Mary's life was a nightmare. She was existing in a state of heart-breaking anxiety. Sometime early in January 1840, she was allowed again, with one of her daughters, to visit John in prison. John was described as emaciated by people who saw him at this time. He had been unwell before the Rising and on that day had spent the best part of twenty-four hours in wet clothes. Her concern for his health was another cause of anxiety.

John's trial for high treason took place in Monmouth between 31st December and 8th January.[97] He pleaded not guilty. John was described in the newspapers as 'cool and collected' and it was noted that 'he paid great attention'.[98] William Davies had gone missing again so could not be called to testify. His account, however, was used in court.

The expectation was that John would be found guilty but as the trial progressed, hopes were raised that he could well be acquitted. The defence was masterly, and the Lord Chief Justice's summing up clearly asked the jury to acquit John. There was reason for optimism. So convinced were some of his friends in Newport that John would be acquitted that excited crowds gathered in the streets, expecting him to arrive on the coach from Monmouth.[99] When, contrary to hope and expectation, a guilty verdict was pronounced on 8th January, he gave positive directions that none of his family was to see him.[100] Mary was not in Monmouth, so she did not listen to all that was said during the eight days of John's trial. William was there and presumably reported to her, and he would have considered her feelings in the traumatic recounting. But nothing could soften the grim truth: her husband was likely to be executed, and soon.

William had his own difficulties. At the time of the trial, he was informed he was to be tried for obtaining upwards of £20,000 (over £1m today) by false pretences. He argued this was being done to distract attention from the defence of his clients and the timing certainly seemed to make this excuse plausible.[101] Mary seems to have believed his explanation.

For the next six months, along with everything else, William's forthcoming trial was hanging over them. John advised Mary not to let William take control of her finances. If only she had listened! But in John's absence, her eldest son was the person she needed to rely on. And he had worked hard to achieve that status. What Mary was unaware of, as she had handed money to William at his urging, was that he would not repay the Frosts' bank overdraft to save her property, nor would he pay the money to the defence lawyers. At that time, John's fate was uppermost in her mind.

The trials of Zephaniah Williams and William Jones, fellow leaders of the Rising, followed. They too were found guilty and so on 16th January, the judges put on their black caps and the three prisoners were sentenced to be hanged and quartered. All three waited together in the condemned cell.

But there was a thread of hope which John's defence lawyers were pursuing, and Mary must have clung to this possibility. She would also have been aware that, throughout the country, Chartists were highly active with rallies, meetings, collections and petitions. Feargus O'Connor, head of the national movement, was editor of the *Northern Star*, the foremost Chartist paper. He had been in Monmouth to follow the trials and had given £100 (£6,000 today) of his own money for the defence. He also tried hard to keep John's name in the public eye while efforts were being made to get the death sentences commuted.[102] Some of the leading Chartists in London were collating all the signed petitions from everywhere in the country to present to the Queen.[103]

The delay caused by the arguments around the technical legal issues proved to be good for John, despite the agony that he and his two fellow Chartists suffered in their condemned cell. For twelve days, the three men waited. Mary, too, waited and the other wives and families. It was assumed the death penalty would be carried out on Thursday 6th February but enough doubt surrounded the verdicts to mean the authorities eventually deemed it advisable to commute the capital sentences. They were to be transported instead. This decision was made behind closed doors and was not known to Mary.

Also unknown to Mary was that, on the night of 2nd/3rd February, the prisoners were swiftly taken to Chepstow and early on Monday 3rd February put on a ship.[104] There were very few witnesses. When did Mary know? It is possible the ship they were on was going down the Bristol Channel and passing Newport before Mary was informed. But the news spread like wildfire.[105] Once the death sentences were commuted and they had been removed from gaol, there was intense pressure for a free pardon. Numerous petitions were submitted asking for clemency. The one from Bath, for instance, contained nine thousand signatures and from Trowbridge, four thousand.[106] William presented his personal petition setting out his view of the irregularities in the trial. The young Queen's forthcoming marriage on 10th February seemed to many to be a chance for clemency. There was still hope. Mary must have clung to this. He was alive, at least, but what she did not know then was that nearly all of the rest of her life was to be dominated by her efforts to get him pardoned.

The Charter newspaper stated that Mrs Frost and her four daughters, presumably Elizabeth, Catharine, Ellen and Anne, were expected in town, i.e. London, on Saturday 8th February, to present a petition to the Queen in person.[107] This seems highly unlikely. Would the family of a traitor be allowed anywhere near the Queen? Meanwhile, William was in London still doing his best for John and trying to get reliable news for Mary. He went to the Home Office where Lord Normanby told him that John was on a ship headed for Portsmouth. Normanby gave permission for William and other family members to visit him there.

John and his fellow prisoners reached Portsmouth on Saturday 15th February. He wrote to Mary the following day, telling her that he was in the dark regarding what the government intended doing with them. He had hoped that the Queen's marriage would be an occasion when a pardon could be granted but he was beginning to despair. He added, 'I have erred, My Dear, greatly erred, it cannot be denied and I am not ashamed to own it.' He told her that anyone who wished to see him would have to gain permission and that his correspondence would be read by the Governor.[108]

John was at a low ebb but the family felt there was still hope of a pardon. The speed of his removal from Portsmouth, however, meant only William managed to see him before he sailed from Britain. William visited him twice on Thursday 20th February to discuss a petition from the family and he promised to return the following Wednesday.

On 26th February, William wrote to the *Morning Chronicle* which printed his letter on the 27th. He began by describing the dreadful condition of the prisoners when he saw them in Portsmouth. No doubt this was not news to Mary as William would surely have told her directly. John's sad circumstances, his depression and ill health were a source of great sorrow to her. William included in the correspondence the text of the petition drafted by him and sent to the Queen on behalf of Mary, John's mother and the children. In it, the family said they are 'bereaved and heart-broken'. It is signed by Sarah Waters, Mary Frost, Elizabeth Frost, Sarah Fry, Catharine, Ellen, Henry and Anne Frost, and was conveyed by William to Lord Normanby at the Home Office on 24th February for him to present to the Queen. Lastly William included the negative reply from Lord Normanby.[109]

When the ship sailed on 25th February, that seemed to dash all hope of John returning home soon.[110] But then it had to put into Falmouth for repairs. John wrote to Mary from the *Mandarin* convict ship in Falmouth on 28th February 1840.[111] He began the letter urging her not to consider following him out to Van Diemen's Land (Tasmania). He had been advised that this would be imprudent. She and the family were among friends in Newport and could look to them for sympathy and protection. He was keen for her to continue to run the business. Although he knew she wanted to join him, her duty lay in caring for their family and that was best done at home. He urged her not to follow him but to show her affection for him in her care for the children. He still believed he would be exonerated and allowed home. His devotion to her and the family shines through. John was still hoping for a free pardon as the ship sailed from Falmouth on 28th February, before many of the petitions on his behalf had been presented.

On 1st March the *Southern Star* printed a letter of sympathy and encouragement to Mary from the citizens of Paisley. It promised petition after petition, meeting after meeting. Mary's reply was printed in full:

Newport, Monmouthshire, March 4th 1840.

My Kind Friends, —Accept all which I have to give, my warmest thanks, for your feeling and sympathising address. I do indeed stand in need of all your condolence. I have lost one of the best and kindest husbands—my poor children one of the best fathers—society one of the best men— and the country one of its most sincere and disinterested patriots.

Oh! could you see the desolation this cruel and unjust sentence has produced in our once happy family, you would say your sympathy was not thrown away. Justly does that talented and rich paper the Northern Star, say, "If Frost had been a murderer or a felon, the benefit of the doubt which existed would have been acceded to him; but it is useless for a political offender to look for anything like justice in this unhappy country." If our oppressors could be satisfied with banishing my dear husband, I then could have gone with him, and shared his fortunes; but no, they considered even that too much lenity for a political offence. It was my intention to follow with my family, but a letter I received from him points out the ruin that would attend such a plan; so that I am obliged to abandon the idea altogether. I must now leave him in the hands of his God and his country; and may a kind and overruling Providence direct and crown your efforts, and restore to me my beloved husband, is the earnest prayer of your obliged,

But deeply afflicted friend,

M. Frost.

P. S. —Too much praise cannot be given to that truly patriotic friend to freedom, Feargus O'Connor, for his untiring exertions in favour of the prisoners. I hope God will reward him—I never can. MF[112]

Meanwhile the idea that Mary could have an audience with the Queen, the proposal put forward in the *Northern Star* in February, was believed by many to be a real possibility. Mary was said to have given her consent, 'if it was the will of the people', and the Bath Female Radical Association had offered to raise the money for her expenses.[113] Money was also offered 'to be applied for the purpose of raising a court dress to Mrs Frost to admit her into the presence of Majesty'.[114] Of course, this was clutching at straws; she never met the Queen.

In March, their Newport Chartist friends organised a petition with the names headed by Edward Frost, John's uncle, and John's friend of twenty years, William Townsend.[115] Throughout the country, meetings were being held and petitions drawn up. In 1840, petitions were received from cities, towns and villages, from large groups and from individuals. For instance, at least four arrived from groups in Bristol and dozens from individuals. In many Chartist meetings held to drum up support for subscriptions or signatures for petitions, the unhappiness of Mary and her daughters was mentioned.

William's Pontypool house was sold that month. He was now living in Bristol where he had tried to revive his solicitor's practice. Surfacing, however, were damning allegations that he had overcharged John's defence fund.

There was a flurry of letters between Mary and Feargus O'Connor of the *Northern Star*, who later described William in the worst possible terms. Mary must have known the flaws in her son's character, but he was her son, her first-born, who had supported her through the nightmare of the previous months. He had done more that anyone for John when he was facing the death penalty so this accusation was deeply painful. But Mary was forced to admit to herself that William was a swindler, that he had robbed the defence fund and quite probably other people as well.

Another man in dire financial difficulties was Sarah's husband, Harry Fry. On 19th May, he was declared bankrupt, later claiming his association, through Sarah, with John and the Chartists had ruined his business. Sarah was close to her family and came more and more to depend on her grandmother, mother and sisters.

How they all felt on 25th May, John's birthday, has to be imagined. They had not seen him since a prison visit in January. His health, they knew, was extremely poor. He had been at sea for three months. Perhaps on that day, they reflected that, just a year ago, they had attended the huge Blackwood rally where John's prestige and influence were riding high. Their concern then had been for Vincent, Edwards, Dickenson and Townsend in Monmouth Gaol. How long ago that must have seemed.

The *Monmouthshire Beacon* reported on 13th June 1840 that a Chartist meeting was held in Caerleon. Its purpose was to submit a petition for John's pardon. The speakers were from Bristol and one of Mary's daughters was also present, although it does not state which one. A tea party followed which suggests there were other women present. Perhaps they were friends from the Newport Female Patriotic Association. The Frosts were still committed to Chartism and family members were becoming celebrities within the movement. The connections between the Chartists in Bristol and Newport were clearly continuing.

That same paper carried another article of interest. It described a Newport Sunday Schools rally in which teachers and children processed up Stow Hill to the fields at the top. There they sang and listened to a talk by the Rev Byron. Were any of the Frost women helpers on that day or did they prefer not to go up Stow Hill but wait in Hope Chapel for the children to return for their tea?

CHAPTER 13

July–December 1840

In July William arranged the sale of his mother's home and business premises. It is astonishing that Mary allowed him to do this. A man with such a poor reputation for financial probity who she knew had cheated her before. Feargus O'Connor wrote a few years later regarding the annuity Mary cashed in for John's defence and surely about William:

> '… she was most inhumanly and unnaturally choused out of several hundred pounds for the purposes of the defence, by one who should have put a guinea in her pocket; rather than take a penny out of it.'

Since January, the charge of obtaining £20,000 by false credit had hung over him. Mary must have found it hard to accept that, although he was clever, articulate and confident, he was also untrustworthy. Not long afterwards he was arrested and refused bail. For a while, he was in a lock-up in Mill Street in Pentonville prior to being taken to Monmouth for his trial. Mary was never to see him again.

His trial took place on 12th August in the County Assizes in Monmouth. William was accused of 'Forgery of a Promissory Note'. He believed there was a strong prejudice against him because of his defence of John and the mention of his stepfather made him very tearful. One of his defence lawyers was a man with whom he had

MARY FROST

become acquainted at John's trial, Sergeant Talfourd. He was a radical MP and a literary man, associate of the Romantic poets and close friend of Charles Dickens. Indeed, Dickens had dedicated to him his 1837 work, *The Pickwick Papers*. Despite the efforts of this literary barrister, William was found guilty and sentenced to transportation for twenty years. His wife was able to see him before he left but there is no record that Mary did. It was a further agony for Mary to have another son so far away and so soon after the loss of her husband. The prison ship sailed on 11th September. The record book of convicts on board *Lord Lynoch* provides us with a detailed description of William:

> *Height 5ft 6½ins, age 33, complexion florid, head oval, hair black (nearly bald), whiskers black, visage oval, forehead high, eyebrows black, eyes brown, nose medium, mouth small, chin small dimpled.*

And what of the Frost family's erstwhile friend, William Davies? He was living in London and writing letters, one of which has survived, to his relatives in Cardiff. Were there other letters written to the family and maybe to Ellen especially, which have not survived? He returned to his parents in Blackwood in November. Amazingly, no charges were ever brought against him. The authorities chose not to, it seems, because doing so would have made it harder to maintain calm.

The Times of 28th September carried a report of a ceremony which was held in Newport a few days earlier, to honour Thomas Phillips, the mayor who had been injured in the Rising. All the gentry and anti-Chartists in the area gathered for an afternoon of self-congratulation. He was presented with a very valuable service of plate, the centrepiece of which was an ornate candelabra. I suppose the only scrap of consolation for the Frosts in all this backslapping was that Thomas Prothero was said to be upset that all the glory was heaped on his junior partner and protégé. But I suspect Mary was way beyond caring about that.

In the course of that devastating year, both Mary's husband and her eldest son had been transported, she had lost her business and been reduced to poverty. And that was not the end of Mary's suffering. On 22nd October, her eldest daughter, Mary Lawrence, died.[116] She had now lost both her Geach children. Mary's widowed husband sent their little daughters, Mary, Anne and Henrietta, to a boarding school in Usk. The tide of grief which must have enveloped her would have made settling into a new home an impossible task. But Mary was a strong woman and for the first time, emerging from John's shadow, she took charge of her life herself. She was able to use her own judgement to reject some of John's advice and do what she thought was best for the family. There was no longer a father, uncle, husband or adult son to direct her actions. By early November, the family had left Newport.

Many papers carried the news that the *Mandarin* with the three Chartist prisoners aboard had arrived safely in Hobart on 1st July but there was no information regarding their health or prospects.[117] Mary must have been calculating how long it would take for John to write and how long after that for a letter to arrive. Meanwhile, rumours and hearsay continued to follow them as Mary and the family were still a newsworthy topic. John's notoriety meant they became news too and the subjects of gossip, despite Mary's wish to remain in the background. Interest in them was intense. Amongst other information the *Glamorgan, Monmouthshire and Brecon Gazette* and the *Merthyr Guardian* gossiped that John's daughters were 'beautiful girls' and that he had two sons, one of whom was in America.[118] Portraits of John were being produced and advertised. A full report of the trial was soon printed and for sale.[119] All the accounts of the Rising were written by men – and nearly all by men hostile to Chartism.

A short paragraph appeared in the *Monmouthshire Merlin* on 31st October 1840, stating that Mary was in financial difficulties and having to rely on charity. Her daughters were said to be leaving home to earn their own living. This was firmly denied. Reports in the *Glamorgan, Monmouthshire and Brecon Gazette* and the *Merthyr Guardian* stated, 'Mrs Frost and her family are in easy if not affluent circumstances and not destitute as is rumoured.'[120] *The Cambrian* said, 'Mrs Frost is not destitute.'[121]

In the *Bristol Times and Mirror* on 14th November, the following was printed:

> *A paragraph which has within the last week gone the round of the papers, asserting that the wife and family of the Chartist Frost had been reduced to a state of pinching indigence, is altogether incorrect. The fact is, Mrs. Frost and her family are now residing at Montpelier, near the entrance into Bristol, from the Gloucester road, in a respectable house, and apparently in easy circumstances. Her son, who was influenced by his misguided father at the Newport riots, has been placed with a chemist, in Bristol, and the second of four daughters, now residing with Mrs. Frost, is about to proceed to France, for the purpose of completing her education, to qualify her for the situation of Governess.*

Other papers were cruel, accusing her of selling the business against her husband's wishes and pocketing the money.[122] Further rumours suggested the money from the sale had been pocketed by William. To Chartists all over the country, however, Mary was a heroine. As well as money being raised for her, very many couples were naming their baby daughters Mary in her honour.[123]

John had wanted her to stay in Newport where he felt the family would receive support. What motivated her to move away? A letter she wrote to the Birmingham Chartist Association the next summer provides an answer. The Chartists in Birmingham had heard the conflicting reports of Mary's financial circumstances and therefore, before raising money for her, they decided to ask her directly to explain her situation. Her reply is worth quoting in full.

4 Montpelier, Bristol, June 26, 1841

DEAR SIR,

I beg the Committee will accept my thanks for their kind inquiries into the state of my pecuniary affairs. I can have no hesitation in making them acquainted with the state of my circumstances, for I am not ignorant of the efforts and exertions they are making on behalf of my injured and beloved husband.

The property alluded to are certain premises in Newport, which bring me in £45 per annum; the deeds of these premises were placed in the hands of our bankers for the sum of £200 in the year 1836; at that time we kept no banking account; but Mr. Frost wanted that sum then, so borrowed it of the bankers, and placed his deeds in their hands. We then opened an account with them; sometimes the balance was in our favour, at other times, in their favour. However, at the time of our calamity, there were £270 due to the bankers. I was advised to sell off our stock, which I did, and at a great sacrifice, as you may suppose. Our prosecutors gave us but little time with their Special Commissions, &c. I did sell off, and paid off every one to whom we were indebted. I also sent for our banking book, and was fully prepared to pay them. They delayed sending their account, and I was called upon by the lawyers to advance money for the defence of my dear husband, under a promise that it was all to be refunded as soon as the Defence Fund could be made available. I did advance, to the amount of nearly £400, one hundred I had refunded, and no more. I quitted my house, left Newport, and came to reside in Bristol, until, as I thought, the storm should have blown over. When I came here, I was in daily expectation of receiving back my money. I was also told that the bankers were paid, but when too late I found my money was all gone the bank not paid, and to crown my afflictions, that £1000 had been drawn from the French funds of my money; in short that all my money was gone. I mention this in justification of my leaving Newport with a large family, when I ought to have remained and recommenced business, which I should have done, had I been permitted to keep what I had. I was invited to London, to Glasgow, to Merthyr, with a promise of support in business, but I could not commence anywhere without a capital, consequently, I chose to remain here with a very limited income, in preference to struggling with the business, without the means of carrying it on as I used to do. One consolation I have, and that is my dear and beloved husband is in happy ignorance of all this. You probably will and may naturally ask me who has been the cause of all this wrong? This is a soro [sic] and tender place to touch. I must decline answering, and I know you will excuse me. This I must tell you, it was not Mr. O'Connor. He had nothing to do with my advancing money for the defence; but you will see that advancing money for the defence, rendered me incapable of paying our bankers. This is the money the country is now called upon to pay, for if the bankers sell the property, I shall be snipped indeed. I sincerely hope that Mr. Rogers, of London, has received the sums which I have seen acknowledged in the Star, and then I hope that that trouble will soon be removed from my mind.

In conclusion, I beg once more to tender my grateful thanks to the committee for their kind sympathy, and for the interest they take in my welfare. I received from Birmingham £3 some time ago. The manner in which it was sent enhanced its value; at the same time I can never have an objection to its being noticed publicly when necessary. It was very acceptable, and I felt much obliged for it, and should there be at any future time anything to send, if it was but 5s., I should prefer its being sent direct to me, for then I should have an opportunity of returning my thanks to the parties who send, and there would be no delay.

With my kind respects to the committee,

I beg to remain, respectfully,

Dear Sir,

Yours obliged,

M FROST.

The shame at her son William's crimes was increased by her knowledge that he had robbed her, and, as it later became clear, the defence fund too. It had taken Mary many months to admit to herself the truth of William's character and because she still found it hard to admit it to others, it allowed the contradictory accounts of her financial situation to persist. And William was not only a liar and a cheat in financial matters, but he also had another secret - a mistress, Louisa, who went by the name of 'Mrs Foster'. They had a daughter, Helen Louisa Harris Foster, who was born in Clifton in March 1839.[124] Helen Louisa was another granddaughter for Mary, but did Mary ever know? Helen and her mother lived near the Frost family in Bristol until at least 1844. It is possible that before William was transported, he confided in Mary and maybe asked her to support his second family.

Was this another reason she chose to move to Bristol? It was a city with which Mary had connections and she suggests she was offered help to settle there. In addition, Bristol was a centre of Chartist activities.[125] It had a Female Patriotic Society,[126] a newly formed Young Men's Charter Association,[127] the Bristol Democratic Harmonic Society, a Chartist choir, and a Chartist Co-op.[128] The Newport Working Men's Association had originally been an offshoot of the Bristol Association[129] and Chartist speakers from both areas were regularly invited to one another's meetings. Mary may well have given hospitality to these Bristol members as she had done for Henry Vincent. It appears her Bristol Chartist friends offered her the support she needed.

And there might have been a further reason: a desire for the anonymity which a large city could give her and her family.

So it was in Bristol that she ended what was possibly the worst year of her life. Although she planned to return to Newport, she had, in fact, left her home town for good.

CHAPTER 14

1841

John's longed-for first letter from Van Diemen's Land, written from Port Arthur on 21st July 1840, finally arrived in the New Year 1841.[130] It was a letter which would have cheered her.

For the sake of his family, John was putting a brave face on things. It was full of expressions of endearment: 'my dear Mary', 'my love', 'my dear'. Contrary to his expectations, the voyage had done him good and his health was excellent. His spirits were better than he expected. He described the journey and his first days there in detail, then went on to state that 'our situation is one of comfort compared with that of many prisoners here' and that they had been treated favourably and 'these were instructions from the highest authority'. He knew his family and friends would be very anxious about him as they must have been imagining hardships and suffering. He told her this as he knew his friends and fellow Chartists would be angry if they heard he was on the chain-gangs and treated as the 'vilest of the vile'. He clearly meant this information to be shared. He hoped his anxiety about them was also unfounded. He was 'anxious, very anxious, to hear of the welfare of my dear children'. He would have known all his correspondence was read, probably in both countries, so that constrained him but his love for Mary is clear. He included advice to her on fortitude and faith.

The relief of this good news must have been great and Mary and the family evidently saw no problem with spreading it. Soon after it was received, Henry Frost spoke at a meeting in Merthyr, reading out his father's letter. He read it, too, on 9th January 1841, at a meeting of the Bristol Chartists which was held to petition the Queen to grant a frcc pardon to John. There were four to five hundred people present.[131]

The family was completely unprepared for the shocking political uproar which followed. The letter, edited to exclude personal material, was printed in *The Times* on 13th January. The full version was printed in the *Northern Star* on the 16th. The letter provoked outrage in the press and in Parliament. John later said one of his daughters had given it to the press. But however the papers, and John's adversaries, had obtained it, it was a disaster. There was a debate in Parliament on the apparent special treatment received by John, Zephaniah Williams and William Jones in Van Diemen's Land. Mention was made of Henry reading his father's letter at a Chartist meeting. There was much criticism of the favour shown to John and the other two Chartist leaders.[132] And although such favour was denied, it led to a drastic change in John's situation. Further letters from John to Mary were carefully kept private.

In Newport in January, as a sign of continued support for the Chartist movement, a huge meeting of men and women from a wide area called for the liberation of the prisoners. Money was also raised by the Frosts' Newport friends to offset Mary's debts.[133] Debates on the fate of the Newport Chartists would be a frequent topic of discussion in Parliament in the 1840s. Twice, motions were submitted in the Commons to present an address to the Queen asking for their pardon; once by Thomas Duncombe MP in 1846, and once by Chartist leader,

O'Connor in 1848. Each must have given the family hope and, as each was defeated, bitter disappointment.

The 1841 census allows us to place the characters in this account with accuracy. Mary was living in Upper Montpelier Road, Clifton, with Elizabeth, Ellen, Anne and one servant. She had given the enumerator the information that she had 'independent means'.

Their home in 4 Montpelier Buildings, at the top end of what is now Richmond Road, had been built in 1823 in the increasingly fashionable, semi-rural, elevated suburb. Its space and fresh air attracted many affluent Bristol residents who preferred it to the older, overcrowded city centre. Having stated that, the disposal of sewage at that time was just as primitive as in Newport, there was no street lighting and Mary would have shared a well and communal pump for water. [134] Now this beautiful suburb with its elegant Georgian buildings is a conservation area and numerous houses are listed buildings. [135]

Her son, Henry, was lodging at 151 Gallowgate, Glasgow. Earlier in the year, Mary had written to a Scottish Chartist, George Ross, a boot and shoe manufacturer with a business in Princes Street, to ask whether he could find a position for Henry in a medical establishment. Ross had found an apprenticeship for Henry in Glasgow Old Apothecary Hall. [136]

Her daughter Sarah, Harry Fry and their son Dennis were still living in Newport and John's mother, Sarah Waters, was living with them. John had hoped that Mary would take his mother into her household but this apparently never happened. Perhaps she did not want to move to Bristol.

Mary's daughter-in-law, Elizabeth Geach and her grandson Herbert were living in Abergavenny. It appears they did not go with William to Van Diemen's Land. It is possible she and William were estranged. She must have felt the disgrace of her husband's crimes and maybe had learned of his mistress and daughter in Bristol. The census record also shows that Mary's granddaughters, the three little Lawrence girls, were in a boarding school in Usk. Mary would have been glad they were together as they would, like her, still be grieving the loss of their mother. The Frost family remained close to the Lawrences and decades later, another generation of Lawrence children was cared for by Anne and Ellen. By 1841, William Davies had returned from London and was living with a cousin in Cardiff. In March 1841, too, the minister, Benjamin Byron, died aged 51.[137] He had been the minister of Hope Chapel for twenty years and had supported the Chartists. This, for Mary, was another loosening of her ties to Newport and her happier past.

Did Catharine, the most adventurous of the Frost women, go to France to train as a governess? She does not appear on the census record, so it is very possible. Emily Brontë was born in 1818, the same year as Catharine. She and her sister Charlotte were also well educated, middle-class women of that time who had to earn their own living as governesses or teachers. They considered going to France but decided on Belgium and arrived in a boarding school in Brussels in February 1842 where they were able to learn French and German. Charlotte wrote about her experiences there in her novels, *Villette* and *The Professor*. Did Mary envy the opportunities of the younger generation? In her youth, the years between the French Revolution in 1789 and the battle of Waterloo in 1815, France was a no-go area.

The daily lives of the Frost family residing in the large city of Bristol would have been becoming settled. The population of Bristol in 1841 was 144,803, compared with Newport's of about 20,000. The variety and number

Montpelier Buildings with number one being the white house on the left (above and below). Number 4 has bow windows. They are now 111-117 Richmond Road. Photos taken 2021

Mary's home, 4 Montpelier Buildings, now 117 Richmond Road
Photo taken in 2021

of shops, theatres, concert halls and meeting places - and the wealth in Bristol - were a far cry from Newport. The fashionable Rennison's Public Baths were on their doorstep and Bristol Zoo close by in Clifton, too. Temple Meads Station opened in 1840, allowing Bristol to be connected to London by rail in 1841. Newspapers from London could be delivered the following morning.[138]

In Newport, they had lived in the heart of the town but in Bristol, they lived over a mile uphill, north east of the city centre. This is not an exceptional distance to walk, especially in those days when everyone but the rich expected to walk wherever they wanted to go. Everyday shopping could be done in their local shopping street. To go further, they could have caught the public omnibus or hired a hansom cab. There were also many Hackney carriages which held four people and had a fixed fare.

The *Monmouthshire Merlin* on 20th March 1841 reported an accident. It appears Harry and Sarah Fry had been to dinner with friends in Machen. As they were returning home in a four wheeled chaise, the horse misbehaved and the chaise overturned, throwing Harry and Sarah into the road. Sarah was unhurt but Harry dislocated his shoulder. Presumably little Dennis's great grandmother, Sarah, was at home with him, along with servants Patience and Ann Pitt. This tumble was perhaps symbolic as, about this time, things started to go wrong with their marriage.

In April, a meeting of the Bristol Chartists was addressed by William Edwards, now released from prison and as fervent as ever.[139] The Frost family were part of this Bristol group, their continuing loyalty to Chartism evident, but there is no indication as to whether any of them were at this meeting, or whether William Edwards brought his wife Sarah and sister Mary Brewer with him. It does seem likely, though.

During 1841, *John Frost, a Chartist Play*, was written and produced about John and the Frost women. It was in blank verse with a five-act structure. For dramatic effect, Mary was shown as being against her husband's Chartism and unhappy at her husband's actions. A footnote explained that this was 'not true in reality'. For added romance, the playwright has Vincent fall in love with one of the Frost daughters. Who played the parts in performances is difficult to imagine, as actors and actresses were not considered respectable and even amateur dramatics were frowned upon, as can been seen in Sir Thomas Bertram's violent reaction to play-acting in Jane Austen's *Mansfield Park*. But *John Frost* had a number of amateur performances in Chartist venues at which money was raised for Mary. The playwright, John Watkins, was invited to speak at a Chartist meeting in Bristol but he declined the offer, so Mary probably never met him.

In June 1841, Henry returned home. He had been doing really well in Glasgow and was highly regarded. He was described as remarkably intelligent and having a strong resemblance to his father. His employers were reluctant to lose him, but his health was deteriorating, and the cold Scottish weather was exacerbating his condition.[140] What a sad disappointment for everyone.

Henry Vincent was eventually released from prison and continued his work as a Chartist missionary in the West country. He began editing the *National Vindicator*. He spoke at a Chartist meeting in Broadmead, Bristol on 21st December 1841, along with Feargus O'Connor.[141] They visited Mary's home on that occasion which was the first time O'Connor had met Mary. He later wrote about 'her sweet family' and 'three most lovely daughters'. He described Henry Frost as being extremely ill.[142] The Frost women were at the meeting to hear Vincent and O'Connor speak. The family were spotted in the gallery and described by the *Monmouthshire Merlin* as 'a very respectable elderly lady accompanied by three rather handsome young females'.[143] If Catharine was in France, then the three young women were probably Elizabeth, Ellen and Anne. Mary and her daughters clearly had a certain celebrity status among Chartists as the advance notices for this meeting, and others, mentioned they would attend.[144]

CHAPTER 15

1842–1844

Mary would, sadly, have been prepared when, on 22nd March 1842, her dearest son, Henry Hunt, died at only eighteen years of age. He had suffered a lingering illness, the death certificate giving the cause as 'Decline' which could be one of any number of conditions. Vincent claimed he died of grief at the separation from his beloved father.[145] He died at home amongst his family at Upper Road, Montpelier, St Pauls. The informant was Thomas Crosby, a solicitor living in the St Paul's area. Could he have been an old friend of William? Or a member of the Bristol Chartists?

Henry was buried at Holy Trinity Church, Wellington Hill, Horfield on 29th March. It was about a mile from their home.[146] Presumably this churchyard was the appropriate one in their locality. It can hardly have consoled Mary as this church was not only Anglican but was High Anglican, ie Anglo-Catholic. Its decorated interior would have been very different from the plain interior of a chapel she was used to.

Henry's death was widely reported throughout the country. There were many sermons, orations, tributes at meetings and collections for funeral expenses. Some described him as the second son of John Frost and others the only son.[147] Henry's death was the most terrible sorrow for Mary. Her husband and eldest son were in Van Dieman's Land, her son John had long gone,

The interior of Holy Trinity, Horfield. Photo taken in 2020.

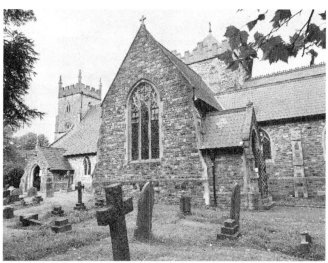

The churchyard of Holy Trinity Church, Horfield
Photo taken in 2020

and little James had died before his first birthday. Now her final, precious boy, the only one of her sons to have embraced Chartism enthusiastically, was gone too. Henry was her husband's hope and joy and so, in addition to her own grief, was the knowledge of how the loss of Henry would affect John. He had missed Henry's babyhood while he was in prison and had missed the last eighteen months of his life, too. With Henry's death, there were only women left in the family. In their mourning clothes, they continued their campaign for a pardon for John.

When Mary had cashed in an annuity over two years previously to contribute towards the defence fund, she had been promised this money would be repaid to her. This promise was kept. On 30th April 1842, an audited account of the funds raised for Mary was published in the *Northern Star*. It stated that in January 1842 £250 (£15,000 today) was deposited with the West of England Bank 'in full discharge of their claims on the estate of Mrs Frost'. By this time, people understood it was her son William who had reduced her to destitution, forcing her to rely on charity.

While the main concern for the women of the Frost family was John, as Chartists they would have been aware that a second attempt to present a petition for the Charter to Parliament was the focus of the nation's Chartists. This second petition was reported to contain three and a quarter million signatures and to be six miles long. In May, Parliament again rejected it. This led to serious rioting in the north of England. Only once more was an attempt made, in 1848, and it was again rejected.

If that news was dispiriting, more affecting would have been the news reaching them about the consequences of the controversy regarding John's letter. *The Cambrian* of

16th June printed an extract from a letter dated Port Arthur, 14th December 1841:

> *Frost, Williams, and Jones are in this settlement. Frost has been sent to Hobart Town to stand a trial respecting some letters he sent to England, which were published in the newspapers and got to the ears of the Government; so he has been sent to this settlement to hard labour. He has done a great deal of harm to himself, as he was very well off before, being employed as a clerk in the commissariat's office, but now he will be at hard labour for some time.*

Other newspapers carried the same account. Mary, doubtless, did not need the papers to know this but it must have amplified her distress. Allowing Henry to read her letter to so many people must have haunted her, but it seemed at the time as if that was what John wanted. She would have been receiving news in regular letters from John, but their letters never reached the press again.

That summer of 1842, there were some happy family events. On 22nd July, Ellen married William Davies. The *Bristol Times and Mirror* states the marriage took place at King Street Chapel. This was a non-conformist chapel in the parish of St Paul's, Bristol, a large, handsome building with a fine organ. It had been registered to solemnise marriages in 1840. The witnesses were her sister, Elizabeth Frost, and William Prowting Roberts, the Bath solicitor who had been arrested in Blackwood in November 1839 seeking to help John. Were they then all reconciled to William Davies? Maybe Ellen was determined and Mary could not refuse her, especially as getting John's permission would have been impractical. Mary believed in Christian forgiveness and events had taught her pragmatism. William Davies's family and the

Frosts had been friends for decades until his inexplicable betrayal at the time of John's trial. Was that now put behind them as they welcomed the addition of a young man into their family? He was clearly close to the Frost women. Not only did he marry Ellen but they invited Elizabeth to be a witness at their wedding and to help them when, after their marriage, they ran a shop in Blackwood. He also in later years accompanied Catharine to Australia. This was the second of his daughters' weddings John did not attend.

Another marriage in Bristol that summer was that of Jane Dickenson who had been a leader in the Newport Female Patriotic Society in 1839. She married an Irishman, Michael Horrigan. Once married, they returned to Newport where they ran a butcher's shop in Commercial Street, and later at 41 High Street. There is evidence of their continued involvement with Chartism in the town as her husband became a subscriber to the Chartist Land Plan.[148]

Other good news for Mary was that, in Newport, Sarah had safely given birth to another baby, a girl. Little Fanny Mary Fry, who was to play such a lasting part in the lives of the Frost family, was born on the 11th August.

The newspapers in September carried an article written by someone who had seen John. He said that John had told him that he would not bring his family out to Van Diemen's Land without seeing a clear way for their provision.[149] At that time, he was a labourer. It appears that he had been ill in hospital but he asked that a message be given to Mary, letting her know he was well. Was his illness connected to the news he must have received that summer about the death of his dear son Henry?

Reports were emerging in November that William Foster Geach was suffering greatly in Van Diemen's

Land. He was living in hope that friends at home could help him, as he wrote that he would rather be dead.[150] It is possible to imagine what a shock his new situation was for someone like William and how difficult it would be for him to bear. There was nothing Mary could do and surely she, after being treated so wickedly by him, would have scant sympathy.

In January 1843, there was a visit by a female Chartist, Mary Ann Walker, to Bristol to speak at some Chartist meetings. She was twenty-two years old and had been speaking at meetings around the country, creating a media storm. The *Northern Star* found it necessary to describe her 'very graceful bust' before any mention of her political views. The *Monmouthshire Merlin*, true to form, also made many comments about her appearance and demeanour but even though this report was disapproving, it was kinder than most. It added, 'one of the gentle sex - stepping out of her natural sphere, in order to swell the tide of political excitement'.[151] Would the Frost women have applauded her willingness to suffer abuse for a cause she believed in? There is never the slightest hint that any of the Frost women spoke to a public audience. Perhaps John's linguistic ability had been inherited but not practised. They were there and they listened but did not speak.

Ellen Davies gave birth to a daughter, Ellen Ann, on 18th July, another little granddaughter for Mary and welcome news for them all. They were living in Blackwood. None of her legitimate grandchildren at this point was living in Bristol within easy reach. Mary's girls were at school in Usk and her son, John Lawrence, presumably in school, too. Dennis and baby Fanny Fry were with their parents in Newport.

There is no record that William Foster Geach's son, Herbert, went to Van Diemen's Land, or his mother either, although in December 1843 there were reports in the papers that William's wife had followed him out. If she did, she did not remain long. There was almost certainly a 'wife' but whether this was Elizabeth is unclear. John had apparently written to Mary and his daughters telling them that William had been allowed to be hired by his wife as a free servant and asking them to come out and do the same for him as he was now comfortably situated.[152]

From time to time newspapers carried short pieces reporting from someone who had seen John or heard from him. This was third-hand information and Mary would have had more reliable information in her own letters, but if she read the reports, they usually commented that John was in employment and good health. Often they carried conflicting reports. The *Bristol Mercury* of 15th June 1844 carried a report from the *Morning Chronicle* of a letter John sent home, stating the Governor of the settlement was recommending he be set free, although he would have to stay in Van Diemen's Land. If this proved to be so, the family were preparing to join him.

Also that month, the *Monmouthshire Beacon* reported that in every letter Mary sent John, she told him how keen she was to join him, and her daughters, too. He, however, was hoping for a pardon soon so it would not be worth their while. She had therefore given up the idea. 'She is a lady of birth, education and manners and her two daughters, both grown up, are also well educated and accomplished.'[153] Presumably these were Elizabeth and Catharine, although Anne would have been nearly eighteen by then. Chartists throughout the country continued their efforts to petition for a free pardon for John and this support would have strengthened Mary and her daughters.[154]

Some distressing news reached the family in September. Their friend and Newport Chartist, John Partridge, had died. He had been a broken man from the time of the Rising and later imprisonment. Six months later, in the spring of 1845, his daughter Amelia married David Williams, a blacksmith, and settled down to produce her own family, never moving far from where she was brought up. And two other marriages took place that winter. Elizabeth Townsend, Sarah's friend, married John Logan, a Scot who was living in Newport employed as a railway contractor. Her brother, William Anselm Townsend, imprisoned with Henry Vincent, married in St James, Bristol. Did these weddings provide occasions for the Frost family to meet up with the families they had been so close to during 1839?

Another cause for happiness perhaps was that she heard William had written to someone in Pontypool to say he was settled and living in Hobart. It appeared John, also settled, was living near him. John would have written to her about this although she would not have leaked the letters to the papers. Possibly John was still unaware at this time of William's theft of Mary's money.

CHAPTER 16

1845-1849

In September 1845 there was a report in the press that Mary had gone out to join her husband, acting as a matron on a convict ship. This was repudiated by the *Bristol Mercury* which stated, 'Mrs Frost, we learn, is by birth, education and fortune, a highly respectable lady, enjoying the respect of all who know her, and is at the present time residing at Montpelier, Bristol.'[155] It must have been a source of pain and irritation to a reserved woman like Mary to be of constant interest to the press. John's notoriety had thrust her into public notice in a way she cannot have liked. On the other hand, she did not want the interest in obtaining a pardon for John to wane. For the family, Mary especially, John's pardon and permission to return home was of paramount importance.

Chartists throughout the country continued to meet and petition for a free pardon so that he could return. It would have been heartening for the family that so many other people were as focused as they were on John's welfare and pardon. Chartist papers kept John's memory alive and throughout the land, they continued to raise petitions. In March 1846, a motion was presented to Parliament consisting of 249 petitions containing 1,400,000 signatures. Hopes were high until remission of the punishment was again refused.[156]

MARY FROST

It was at about this point that any expectation that Mary and her family would emigrate to join John in Van Diemen's Land was shelved for good. Sometime in the latter half of the 1840s, Mary and her daughters moved to what was to become their permanent home at 30 Stapleton Village, just under two miles east from their previous home. It became known as the Frost House and now has a blue plaque - although the date of John's arrival on it is a year out.

Photos of the 'Frost House' taken in 2020

In Newport, early in 1846, Sarah converted to Roman Catholicism. For over two hundred years after the Act of Uniformity of 1559, outward observance of the Roman Catholic faith had been illegal in England. The building of public places of worship did not resume until late in the 18th century and gathered pace after Catholic Emancipation in 1829. St Mary's Roman Catholic Church at the bottom of Stow Hill in Newport had opened in 1840 with a lavish Pontifical High Mass conducted by the Vicar Apostolic of Wales. Its priests had then set about their pastoral and missionary work in the town and Sarah must have undergone instruction. This was yet another departure from her parents' beliefs and a puzzling one. Was she again trying to distance herself from her parents' way of life? Mary's friends in Hope Chapel and the Chartist movement must have wondered. Was she prepared for the demands the Roman Church would make on her, especially in terms of obedience and religious discipline? The traditional language of Catholic devotion would have been foreign to her, and Catholic forms of worship perhaps dry and unappealing. Some points of doctrine were often hard to accept for converts brought up in the Protestant tradition.

In addition, sometime after her conversion, Sarah's marriage to Harry Fry broke down and she moved into her mother's home, bringing little Fanny with her. Dennis, by now, was away at school. Mary had been giving Sarah money for necessities as, Sarah claimed, Harry would not. Sarah and her troublesomeness had not disappeared when she married. She was to be taxing for the family, especially Mary, for many years to come. She was a woman who made choices which brought her unhappiness. Mary at sixty-four years of age, with a grown-up family, supported Sarah financially and took responsibility for little Fanny. Mary was to look after Fanny for the rest of her life.

Sarah was not the only family member who converted to Catholicism. More surprisingly, her sisters, Elizabeth and Anne, also converted. In Bristol in 1843, the Catholic Church had bought St-Mary-on-the-Quay Church and the first priest was a Franciscan, Fr Patrick O'Farrell. Anne in 1847 and Elizabeth in 1848 were baptised in St-Mary-on-the-Quay, Bristol by Fr O'Farrell.[157] They were confirmed there in 1849. Roman Catholicism is at the far end of the ecclesiastical and theological spectrum from their parents' beliefs. Congregationalism with its self-disciplined, rational ethos, its reliance on individual conscience and private reading of the Bible and its dislike of elaborate ritual and ceremony is a world away from Roman Catholicism, with its saints' days, rituals, confessionals, Latin masses, and celibate religious vocations. This difference in beliefs between Mary and her daughters appears not to have lessened the familial ties between them but cannot have left Mary unaffected. Coupled with the ebbing away of the Chartist movement in the late 1840s, two once fixed points of Mary's life were under question. It will have led to her making some serious mental and emotional adjustments.

In December 1846 William Foster Geach received a conditional pardon although news of this did not reach him until June 1848. It seems clear that the 'wife' he was living with was not Elizabeth from Abergavenny. A report in the *Gloucester Journal* of August 1847 stated that he and his wife were living in Bagdad, twenty-three miles north of Hobart, where she went by the name of Mrs Foster and kept a very respectable boarding school. Could this have been Louisa, William's mistress from his Bristol days, and was their daughter Helen with them? John was said to be living near them. This must have been some comfort to the family at home although they could hardly have approved of William's irregular marital arrangements.

At the end of 1849 and beginning of the new decade, John wrote to Mary informing her he was collecting certificates of character from men in positions of authority in Van Diemen's Land in support of his application to the Governor for a conditional pardon. He must have conveyed to the family his belief that this would be successful. A report reached Bristol from the *Hobart Town Courier* that the Governor planned to recommend that John be freed.

CHAPTER 17

1850–1853

The family, too, did not let up in their efforts on his behalf. Catharine, in April 1850, wrote a petition from them all to Sir George Grey, Principal Secretary of State for the Home Department.[158] The family knew of the very positive testimonials which had been gathered in Van Diemen's Land to present John's case to the Governor, and Catharine used these in her petition to further endorse the family's own affirmations of John's good character. Of his part in the Rising, they stated, 'he was actuated by no selfish motive but that he offended against the law from the delusion of a mistaken enthusiasm seeking to effect what he earnestly thought a good for his country'. They felt it was a 'step he was induced to take'. His family had formed his happiness 'before the spirit of the times seduced him into politics'. Their arguments for his pardon rested on his good character, his age, the sufferings and length of his exile and his separation from his family. Mary was then sixty-eight years old and she and her daughters 'incessantly pine' for John's return. They asked that he consider the suffering of the family 'from the bereavement of their beloved protector and restore him to his deeply attached wife and children'. It was signed by Mary Frost, Elizabeth Frost, Sarah Mary Fry, Catharine Frost, Ellen Davies and Anne Frost.

Petitions, or 'memorials' as they were called, were not personal correspondence but were part of a formal process, used by the Chartists to put forward their requests for change and used extensively by families and friends of prisoners. Their wording tended to be formulaic, pleading different cases along quite similar lines. The Frost women would have been advised on what to say, when it was worth petitioning and with whose support.

It is a tribute to both their parents that their daughters were so loyal and centred on seeing them reunited. They waited for four months, living in hope, until the disappointing refusal was sent on 26th August.

The census of 1851 is more detailed than that of 1841 and shows Mary living in Stapleton, with Catharine, Anne, eight-year-old Fanny Fry and one servant. She described herself as a 'Proprietor of houses'. Sarah was also resident with them but at the time of the census was visiting her friend, Elizabeth Logan, previously Elizabeth Townsend. Being a railway contractor, her husband moved about with his work and at the time of the 1851 census, the family was living in Nottinghamshire. How long Sarah stayed with them we have no means of knowing but she was back with her family by June as she signed a letter there that month. Her estranged husband, Harry Fry, was in lodgings in Upper George Street in Newport. Their son Dennis was away at boarding school and spent his holidays with his father. Fanny presumably attended a day school in Bristol as she was living at home with Mary at the date of the census, 30th March, which was a month before Easter that year and therefore not in the school holidays. The only Bristol girls' school for which 1850s attendance records still exist is the famous Red Maids School and sadly Fanny's name does not appear in them. There were many small private schools whose records have not survived which she could have attended. We know that the school fees for both children were paid for by Harry.[159] It could be that Fanny received some of her education from her grandmother and her aunts. School was not compulsory before 1870.

In 1851, Elizabeth was living away from home with Ellen and William Davies who were running William Davies's father's shop in Blackwood. Elizabeth would be a great help, having spent so much of her life in her parents' business.

By 1851, George Lawrence, husband of her late daughter Mary, had remarried, and their children, John, Anne and Henrietta, were living with George, his second wife and family and four servants in Chepstow Road, Newport. Her eldest granddaughter, Mary Lawrence, was visiting friends in Blaina: a family named Levick whose father was a wealthy ironmaster.

Her eldest grandson Herbert, then calling himself William Henry Geach, was living as a lodger in Birmingham and working as a clerk. Did he feel the need to distance himself and start his professional life away from the area of his father's criminality, a place where the name of Geach was not tainted?

Mary's mother-in-law, Sarah Roberts, was by then aged 91 and living at 2 Thomas Street, Newport, with a nurse. Not long after the census, on 2nd May 1851, she died in her home in Thomas Street. The funeral was held on the 8th at St Woolos. This was another piece of sad news for Mary to send John. It is worth quoting the obituary in the *Bristol Mercury* in full:

> *She was for many years landlady of the Royal Oak where she carried on a large and lucrative business. She was pious, charitable, unostentatious, and just and her memory will*

long be revered by a large circle of friends. This aged lady died with her faculties unimpaired, and in the humble hope of a blessed immortality. She has left considerable freehold property, which descends to Mrs Frost. [160]

Regarding Mary's properties, there was a report in the *Monmouthshire Beacon* of 26th February 1853 about a dispute between the railway company and a number of house owners in Thomas Street, Newport, regarding the placing of a level crossing in Pentonville. Mary, by then, owned five freehold houses and one leasehold house in Thomas Street. She probably had other sources of income, as well. Late in life, she had become financially secure again.

Still desperate to see her father, on 4th June 1851, Catharine wrote on her own account to Lady John Russell, wife of the Prime Minister. She begged her to use her influence with her husband on John's behalf. 'It is to the feelings of the daughter, the wife and the mother I would appeal ...' She referred to John's high moral character and that his age could mean he, 'the being they most love', might die before a reunion 'which is so ardently prayed for by his afflicted family'.

She closed: 'I beg to remain/Most respectfully/Your Ladyship's/very obedient servant /Catharine Frost.'

There is no record of a reply. John Russell would not have forgotten that this was the man who argued with him and mocked him. Back in March 1839, John had written to a Chartist colleague describing how, when campaigning in the Stroud area to win the parliamentary seat from Russell, he had continually scorned and 'hammered at' the aristocratic Russell nicknaming him 'Little Finality'. Russell had since become the most powerful man in the land, and it is heart-breaking that Catharine had to plead with him in such an abject way.

Just a few weeks later, Catharine wrote another petition, this time on behalf of the family, to Sir George Grey, Her Majesty's Secretary of State in the Home Department. Their letter began:

> Sir, In addressing you, sir on behalf of our beloved and long exiled Husband and Father we would do so with all the earnestness the subject inspires and with all the deference and respect due to your position and character.

The petition spoke of the 'deep anguish' suffered by the family and the 'dread which weighs down the spirits' at the thought that he could become ill and die without their care. His hair had become white and his back bent, so they begged for a merciful consideration of his case. It was signed: Mary Frost, Elizabeth Frost, Sarah Fry, Catharine Frost, Ellen Davies and Anne Frost. The negative reply was sent at the end of July.

The petition Catharine wrote on 15th February 1853 had a more desperate tone. The Secretary of State had changed in December 1852, so this final petition written by her was addressed to Lord Palmerston. While repeating many of the arguments included in previous petitions, she reflected on the tremendous efforts made and the numerous letters, prayers and petitions submitted during the previous twelve years to obtain permission for John to return home. She informed him that a petition had been presented by the family last year which had been signed by fifty to sixty MPs. She wrote of the recommendation from the Governor of Van Diemen's Land. All the refusals showed the utter failure of their efforts and had destroyed 'the hope that has been so long cherished'. There was an acceptance in this petition that John would never be allowed to come home and so they requested that he be given a conditional pardon so that he could move to Australia where his family could join him. Her final plea was that a decision could be reached swiftly in consideration of her father's age. It was signed by Mary Frost, Elizabeth Frost, Sarah Mary Fry, Catharine Frost, Ellen Davies and Anne Frost.

A month or so later, so sure were the family that John would be pardoned, Catharine, accompanied by William Davies, set off for Australia. William Davies went perhaps to explore the possibility of emigrating with his wife and daughter; Catharine to be with her father when the expected pardon came through.

But still no pardon was granted, so on 23rd August, Mary herself wrote to Lord Palmerston at the Home Office. She mentioned she was then nearly seventy and concerned that she and John, her 'beloved husband', would not see each other again. She mentioned previous applications made by herself and her daughters and that they had been led to believe mercy would be shown, to the extent that a daughter had already set off four months ago for Adelaide in the hope of meeting her father. She again begged him for an early consideration of their case. She ended her letter, 'I beg to subscribe/Myself very respectfully/Your Lordship's /Humble servant/M Frost'. Again, she waited for a reply.

There was an added worry for the aging Mary in that Sarah was to appear as a witness in court. The *Bristol Mercury* of 26th November 1853 reported on a court case brought by a shopkeeper against Harry Fry for £8 9s (£500 today). This money had been spent by Sarah on clothes. She appeared in court and was described as 'a respectably attired and good-looking woman'. She stated that he had kept her short of money and this was unkind to her. He argued that as she had left him, he was not responsible for her debts. He claimed John's Chartist views and consequent conviction for High Treason had damaged his business. Sarah was again living with the

Logan family, although Fanny remained with Mary. Harry was paying for Dennis's and Fanny's schooling, but Mary was supporting Sarah financially. This public airing of the private lives of her family would have been distasteful for Mary.

CHAPTER 18

1854-1857

Finally, on 7th March 1854, an announcement in the House of Commons granted conditional pardons for John, Zephaniah Williams and William Jones. Mary wrote to John on the 11th.[161] That month, Catharine joined John in Van Diemen's Land. He was then a schoolteacher. Zephaniah Williams' wife Joan, and their daughter decided to emigrate and join Zephaniah,[162] but John just wanted to come home.

As soon as news of a conditional pardon was known, calls were made for a full and free pardon. The *Star of Gwent* of 1st April reported that, at the end of March, there was a large meeting in Newport, called by John's uncle Edward Frost and his long-time friend, William Townsend. Hundreds of citizens, sympathetic to John's situation, attended. Again, a petition was raised, mentioning his good conduct, his suffering and that of his family, 'a fond and beloved wife and faithful and interesting children'. Mary was described as 'a most amiable, pious woman' and her home as 'a harmonious and well conducted household'. The *Monmouthshire Merlin* also reported the meeting at length quoting the words of one attendee about Mary:

> *... she was a good wife, and a good manager;*
> *and I may say she was actually a woman who*
> *tried to tread in the steps of John Frost... consider*
> *the trials and troubles of Mrs. Frost—all she has*

*gone through these fifteen years, shall we not feel
for her also? She is still alive, notwithstanding all
she has suffered...*

Sarah learned in April she had become a widow. Harry
Fry, aged fifty-six, had died. He had continued to live in
lodgings in George Street in Newport after Sarah had left
him. It was usual in those days for businessmen to
insure their lives as a way of ensuring dependants had
money to live on, but of course, Harry may have forfeited
his policy when he became bankrupt. As she had been
living apart from him, his death probably made little
practical difference to Sarah except that it set her free.
Mary's grandchildren, Fanny and Dennis, who had lost
their father, were now wholly dependent on Sarah – or
more probably, Mary.

In July, John and Catharine heard he had received
the conditional pardon and started making plans to leave
Van Diemen's Land. At the end of December, they
departed for the United States, going via Callao in Peru
to California,[163] then on to New York. Letters from New
York to Britain took about twelve days. That was a great
improvement on the two or three months taken by news
to reach home when John was first transported.
Catharine was a keen letter-writer so Mary would have
felt much more in the picture.

In a very strange turn of events in June 1855, an
Italian nobleman, a Marquis, Guiseppe Pasqualino, came
from Palermo in Sicily to Clifton in Bristol to visit the
family of his late wife, the aristocratic and wealthy Mary
Charlton. He was looking for a nurse for their four-year-
old daughter. In Bristol, Sarah had become acquainted
with a doctor, William Austin Gillow, at whose practice
in Clifton she was a patient. Dr Gillow, a well-known
Bristol Catholic,[164] recommended Sarah to Pasqualino.
Was the doctor aware that she was in the early stages of

tuberculosis and considered the Italian climate would be beneficial? Sarah accepted the post and became nurse and governess to little Marietta Pasqualino, returning with them to Sicily where Pasqualino owned a house in Palermo and a country house a few miles beyond it. Members of the snobbish Charlton family were horrified when they discovered she was the daughter of John Frost, as can be imagined.[165] Fanny remained behind with Mary and Anne in a rather depleted household.

Sadly, near the end of 1855, Henry (Herbert) William Geach died in Birmingham where he was employed as a clerk. He was just twenty-four years of age and was Mary's eldest grandson. He had been only eight years old when his father had been found guilty of fraud and transported and so he had been brought up by his mother. Interestingly he was using the name 'Henry', the name of his uncle, Henry Frost, who had died in 1842, rather than his birth name 'Herbert' which presumably was given to him to please his rich cousin Rachel Herbert, whose fortune would probably have been his eventually.

This was another of the great changes that had taken place in the sixteen years since John had left. In that time John's mother Sarah, their son Henry, Mary's daughter, Mary Lawrence, her grandson, Herbert, son-in-law Harry Fry and many friends had died. Also Ellen had married, William Foster Geach had been transported and their granddaughters Fanny and Ellen had been born. All these joys and sorrows that Mary should have shared with John, she had lived through alone.

In March 1856, John was speaking at a meeting in New York. The New Yorkers raised and sent a petition to the Queen for a free pardon.[166] Petitions were being sent from all over Britain, too.[167] Finally, in May 1856, John was granted an unconditional pardon.[168] He could return home. John and Catharine immediately set about arranging their passage. They landed in Liverpool on 12th July.[169] After a few days in London, they went on to Stapleton and home. Mary had not seen him for over sixteen years. His hair was white and Mary's, too, I would imagine. Neither of them had had an easy time. Theirs was a relationship kept alive by correspondence. They were not the same people they had been. Reunions, especially after such a long time, are rarely uncomplicated. There is no record of this, surely highly emotional, meeting. But he was certainly glad to be home and she was certainly very glad to see him. It was a day they had feared would never come.

Mary now begins to fade from the record. John still had energy, ambition and unchanged radical views. He resumed his family position centre stage and perhaps, from her point of view, he had never really left it. In John's shadow again, she retired into the background, where, I think, she felt happiest. He had to get to know his daughters again and they him. The youngest, Anne, was, by then, thirty. He had to meet his granddaughter Fanny who was then nearly the same age as Anne had been when he had left. But before long, he set off to visit old friends and places - his beloved Newport, of course, where he had a rapturous reception,[170] and London, Leeds and others. There is no record of Mary accompanying him. Of course, she did not go with him on his journeyings in 1839, but then she had the shop to manage and children who needed their mother.

He found the world that he returned to had changed radically. South Wales was by then a boom area. All over the country, people's lives had been improved. His great adversary, Thomas Prothero, was dead, as was old Charles Morgan of Tredegar House. Further afield, Feargus O'Connor had died. Chartism was petering out as 'its members followed other paths to a better future'.[171] The population of Newport had doubled and many on the town council had radical sympathies. Mary and his daughters would have prepared him for the changes which had taken place in the town. High Street had been widened and a monument to Charles Morgan had been erected there.[172] Hope Chapel was where it had always been but worshippers now attended a new Congregational chapel which had been built in Dock Street.

By the beginning of 1857, John was hoping to be the parliamentary candidate for Merthyr Tydfil.[173] In September, he was lecturing in Newport. The family in Stapleton, Mary, Elizabeth, Catharine, Anne and Fanny, had no wish to move back to Newport, even though there are hints John would have liked to.[174] They would have been glad to see him in such health and good spirits and they would have looked forward to news when he returned home each time from his visits. But their lives had settled into different patterns.

William Davies also returned from Australia, keen to take his family and settle there. Mary, presumably, was reconciled to her daughter's husband but how did John feel about seeing him again? And what of Sarah in far away Palermo working in the home of the Marchese Guiseppe Pasqualino? Well, reader, she married him. Pasqualino's father was President of the Grand Council of the King of the Two Sicilies. What an amazing change of social position for the daughter of a radical draper from Newport to be raised into the Italian aristocracy. Sarah's second marriage is astonishing but certain. What is not certain is the date the marriage took place. Announcements were placed in the local newspapers with the date given variously as 28th November 1857 and 9th December 1857,[175] but studying the records from

Palermo Cathedral, it is absolutely clear that the date of this marriage was June 1858. Did she write to her mother that she was to be married and the information was misconstrued?

Mary died on 2nd December 1857 at age of seventy-five. Her death certificate gives the cause as 'Congestion of the Brain' which probably means she had a stroke. Her beloved John was with her when she died. She was buried on 9th December in Henry's grave in Horfield, Bristol. It was the end of an era. For the family, the strong and steady point in their lives had gone. Many years later, in 1874, John spoke to a reporter about his past and of Mary he said, 'My dear wife, the very best friend I ever had in my life, God bless her!'[176]

John remained in Stapleton with his daughters, Elizabeth, Catharine, Anne and granddaughter, Fanny. Strangely, there were no announcements of Mary's death in the papers. John's mother's death had prompted a very flowery obituary and Sarah's marriage announcement was placed in a number of papers. Did Mary tell John she did not want anything about herself in the press?

Perhaps Sarah lied about the date of her marriage as she knew her mother was dying and wanted to let her know she was settled. For by marrying Guiseppe Pasqualino, Sarah had made the decision to stay permanently in Italy. And after Mary's death, other family members were also moving away. In September 1858, William Davies returned to Australia with Ellen and their teenage daughter, Ellen Ann. Catharine decided to go with them. So at the time of the 1861 census, just John, Elizabeth, Anne and Fanny were living in the Frost house in Stapleton. Fanny's brother, Dennis Fitzroy Kelly Fry, John's only grandson, was a sergeant with the British Army in Chatham prior to sailing for India. Did John ever meet him? Sometime after the 1861 census, it seemed Elizabeth died and in 1864 Sarah, having given birth to another daughter, Emilia Pasqualino, was dying of tuberculosis.

When John died in 1877, three of their daughters were still living: Catharine, Ellen and Anne. There were also grandchildren: Sarah's three children, Dennis and Fanny Fry and Emilia Pasqualino; Ellen's daughter, Ellen Ann, William's illegitimate daughter, Helen Louisa and Mary Lawrence's children. Some of these went on to have children and grandchildren of their own. Their descendants, in Italy and elsewhere, may have no idea of the family from which they came.

The family grave at Holy Trinity, Horfield, Bristol. This stone was erected in the 1980s.
Photo taken in 2020

CHAPTER 19

Conclusion

In summing up, there is always the danger of over-simplification. This is especially true in the case of little recorded, complex personalities. In the course of her life, Mary developed from the 18th century girl to the mid-Victorian woman, shaped both by her choices and by happenings quite out of her control. All the direct statements which describe her echo the Georgian and Victorian feminine values of respectability and domesticity; included also are her stoicism, education and, of course, class. More than once, she was described as a 'lady'. By nature she was reserved but also strong, resolute and tenacious.

Although running the shop probably allowed her to exercise her abilities much more than many middle-class women of the time who were tied to a solely domestic existence, throughout her life Mary, as far as I can see, never deviated from her traditional female role. The mainsprings of her life were John and the children, her religious faith and Chartism. She always put John first, prioritising his ambitions and activities. She had a flexible rather than rigid personality, allowing her to adapt to changing circumstances. Her faith sustained her, and the radical ideas of the Chartists enlarged her mind. Her strength kept her going through all the suffering and responsibility caused by John's Chartist activities.

CONCLUSION

For her Frost daughters, some of their happiest memories of childhood could have been the great Chartist rallies as they experienced the excitement and promise of the first half of 1839. Did the Rising's failure and the punishment meted out to their father damage their belief in the movement as it damaged their personal lives? They were so often described as a group – 'beautiful', 'handsome', 'accomplished' - as if there were no variations. More than one commentator described them as 'interesting', perhaps a coded suggestion that they had opinions and could hold serious conversations. It also suggests distinct personalities.

It was their misfortune to go through life as John Frost's daughters. They soon learned that their every action and statement would be pounced upon. Even before the Rising, their names were not mentioned among the other females involved in the movement. Like Mary, they kept a low profile. Although the Chartist movement had a lasting impact on their lives, we cannot be sure how committed to Chartism each individual daughter was, either in 1839 or subsequently. Some of them, with Mary, continued to attend Chartist meetings after 1840. But they were five quite different personalities.

Elizabeth was John's eldest daughter and Mary's second. She stood beside her mother as the quiet backbone of the family, the spinster daughter, sister and aunt. She was a witness at the weddings of her stepsister Mary Foster Geach and her younger sister, Ellen. She became housekeeper for Ellen when she and husband William Davies were running a shop in Blackwood. This apart, she was a constant presence with her mother. Her conversion to Catholicism is the only evidence of her having divergent views.

MARY FROST

Sarah, the Frosts' second daughter was the one who appears on the surface to have cared least about family feelings and beliefs. She was the rebel. Her early and ill-judged marriage to the dubious Harry Fry suggests she wanted to be her own woman and the only way she could achieve an identity distinct from the Frost family was to marry. She later needed to be free from him and their marriage. Along with her inability to live within her means, it suggests a woman restless and dissatisfied who made unwise choices and would not be advised.

Her conversion to Roman Catholicism is interesting for it was both a rejection of her parents' beliefs and a commitment to a patriarchal and prescriptive ideology. Going to Italy must have presented itself as another, more exciting, means of distancing herself from her life at home. To do this, she was prepared to leave her daughter, Fanny, and this was only possible because Mary was willing to look after her. She had left Fanny at least twice before when she had gone to visit her friend Elizabeth Logan in Nottingham, but this was a permanent responsibility for Mary. Sarah's son, Dennis, presumably went straight from school into the army.

Status appears to have mattered to Sarah. She was proud of John's position as a Justice of the Peace, including that fact in the announcement of her first marriage. Both of her marriages lifted her up the social scale. She loved clothes and, in this way, reflected her upbringing in a draper's shop. Spending money on clothes was the reason for the court case in which she had to answer for her debts. On that occasion, she was described as 'respectably attired'. When she married Guiseppe Pasqualino, she could have expected to be wealthy but even as a marchioness, she apparently had very little money and was known to wear his first wife's clothes. On her deathbed she was concerned about Fanny's lack of mourning clothes.[177]

She was loyal to her family to some degree. She gave her son the names of her father's defence lawyer, Fitzroy Kelly. Heavily pregnant, she spent at least one evening with her family when John was in prison. She was close to her grandmother, her namesake, who lived with her for a while. She stood with her mother and sisters in signing every document asking for John's pardon. And she relied on her family, especially Mary who supported her emotionally and financially.

Catharine inherited her mother's loyalty but applied it more adventurously. She was a confident, active woman who was restless in a different way from Sarah. It is suggested she went to France to train as a governess. She certainly went to Australia to accompany John home. She toured the States with him. She returned to Australia after her mother's death. When there was something to be done, she did it. She went with her mother and Ellen to see John in the Westgate on 5th November. I suspect she was the daughter who accompanied the reporter to Monmouth Gaol in November 1839. She was the writer of the letters so, alone among them, we hear Catharine's own voice.

Ellen was the only other of the Frost daughters to marry. Like Sarah, she married a dubious man. Eyebrows must have been raised at her choice of William Davies. Like her father, he had been a Chartist and a draper. Ellen, too, was well-versed in Chartism and would have had plenty of experience of how to run a successful draper's shop. While William went to Australia to investigate the possibility of making a life for them there, she, with her daughter, Ellen, lived with her husband's relatives. After her mother's death, she, William and Ellen Ann emigrated.

Finally Anne, just thirteen years old at the time of the Rising, was a woman of thirty when John returned. She was home-loving and loyal. There were no comings and goings in Anne's life: she lived with her mother until her death, then looked after her father until his death in 1877. By then, she was over fifty, her life spent in devotion and service. Her Christian faith, practised first as a Congregationalist and then as a Roman Catholic, was a lasting aspect of her life.

Mary had been schooled to accept that she was second class, and she did accept it. John was a man who took the lead and handed out advice. Curiously, she didn't always take it. She did not create a fuss but quietly went her own way, making her own decisions. She probably surprised herself by how well she managed without John, initially in the 1820s during his imprisonment and then his Chartist travels in 1839, and later when she brought her family through the terrible traumas following the Rising. But she was never happy without him.

Did her daughters accept a second-class status for themselves? They were brought up in a different era. A young female was queen, and she was becoming a role model. They had been encouraged to work in the shop as John was keen for them to be able to earn their own livings. Had Chartism, and their parents' total commitment to it, allowed them to develop aspects of their natures which maybe in earlier times would have been stifled. Did becoming politicised during their formative years enable them to get rid of their Victorian straitjackets? Possibly not. For there was another aspect of Chartism which placed women firmly into a domestic role. In this, it was no different from the traditional restrictive middle-class norms. And their mother's life set an example of this for them.

CONCLUSION

Chartism emphasised families and classes working together towards their goal of a fairer society. At what point did women realise that Chartism's fight against political exclusion was contradictory when it excluded women? How long before they realised that they were working against their own interests and that it encouraged them to stay home rather than enter public life? When later generations of women fought for the right to vote themselves, it was men of their own class, own area and own family with whom they came into conflict. But, even had she lived that long, I cannot see that this would have been possible for Mary - unless John had also embraced the fight for female suffrage and there is no indication that he would have. But their daughters may well have felt differently.

Mary's sons brought her pride and heartbreak but her daughters, without doubt, were sources of much joy. They remained with her or near her for most of her life. She gave them their early education and their model of female being in the world. However much they differed, they all exhibited aspects of her, the Mary who rebelled against the stuffy 18th century politics of the Fosters, the Mary who loved her husband and family, the Mary who bravely survived all the crushing tragedies, Mary the Christian, Mary the Chartist, Mary the home-lover who kept the Frost home going until John returned.

The inner lives of women are often hidden from historians. They have to be imagined. Mary made no claims for herself. She was a strong, quiet and loyal woman. Her life encompassed events of historic importance and those events, over which she had little or no control, caused her years of suffering. If women's roles in Chartism were secondary, then so were their punishments - they did not have to suffer trials, imprisonments or transportation, but endured waiting and hoping, loss and grief. Mary was overshadowed by John in life and after her death was forgotten by history.

I will conclude with the tribute one of the greatest of 19th century writers gave to the subject of her work, as it seems to me it is a fitting tribute to Mary Frost, too. Describing her heroine, Dorothea, another Victorian lady, at the end of her tremendous novel, *Middlemarch*, George Eliot wrote:

> *Her full nature... had no great name on earth. But the effect of her being on those around her was incalculably diffusive: for the growing good of the world is partly dependent on unhistoric acts; and that things are not so ill with you and me as they might have been, is half owing to the number who lived faithfully a hidden life, and rest in unvisited tombs.*

ABOUT THE AUTHOR

Sylvia was educated at Lady Margaret High School, Cardiff, The Western Theological College, Bristol, and Bristol University where she gained a BA and a PGCE. She gained a Masters degree with the Open University, her specialism being Victorian poetry. Her career was spent as a teacher of English in secondary schools in Bristol, Newport and the Valleys.

Since retirement, having more time has meant being able to develop her interests in local and women's history, literature, travel and embroidery. She particularly values the time she spends with her three granddaughters.

This is Sylvia's second book. Her previous book, *Every Woman Remembered,* told the story of the women of Newport in the Great War and was a best seller.

Sources

Books

Charlton, Barbara, *Recollections of a Northumbrian Lady 1815–1866* (1989) Spredden Northern Classics.

Chase, Malcolm, *Chartism: a New History* (2007) Manchester University Press.

Davis, Haydn, *The History of the Borough of Newport* (1998) Pennyfarthing Press, Newport.

Dawson, J W, *Commerce and Custom: A History of the Ports of Newport and Caerleon* (1932) R H Johns.

Evans, Chris, *Slave Wales: The Welsh and Atlantic Slavery 1660-1850* (2010) University of Wales Press.

Humphries, John, *The Man from the Alamo* (2004) Glyndwr Publishing.

James, Les, *Render the Chartists Defenceless* (2015) The Three Imposters.

Jones, David J V, *The Last Rising: The Newport Insurrection of 1839* (1985) Clarendon Press Oxford.

Matthews, James, *Historic Newport* (1910) Williams Press, Newport.

Mills, David, *William Foster Geach* (2015) Stow Park Church Printers.

Mills, David, *William Davies* (2018) Stow Park Church Printers.

Morgan, John, *A Brief Historical Sketch of Bristol* (1849) H & A Hill, Castle Green.

Osmond, David, *Newport and the Chartist Land Plan* (2014) Gwent Local History Journal.

Roderick, Alan, *A Newport Kaleidoscope* (1994) Handpost Books.

Schwarzkopf, Jutta, *Women in the Chartist Movement* (1991) Macmillan.

Scott, J M, *The Ancient and Modern History of Newport, Monmouthshire: with a guide and directory* (1847) William Christophers, Newport.

Thompson, Dorothy, *The Chartists* (1984) Maurice Temple Smith.

Thompson, Dorothy, *The Dignity of Chartism*, Edited by Stephen Roberts (2015) Verso.

Thompson, Dorothy, Editor *The Early Chartists* (1971) Macmillan.

Vaughan, Derrick Cyril, *Newport First Stop* (1990) newportpast.com

Walcott, Ruth/James, Les/ap Hwyell, Elin, Editors, *Voices for the Vote: Shire Hall and the Story of Chartism in South Wales* (2011) Shire Hall, Monmouth.

Wilks, Ivor, *South Wales and the Rising of 1839* (1984) Croon Helm Ltd Publishers.

Williams, David, *John Frost: A Study in Chartism* (1939) University of Wales Press Cardiff.

Wright, Mary, *Montpelier A Bristol Suburb* (2004) Phillimore & Co.

Trades Directories

Pigot & *Co Directory of Monmouthshire* 1822, 1830, 1835 and 1844.

Hunt's Directory 1849.

Matthews Directory of Bristol 1851.

Booklets, Pamphlets and Information Sheets

Chartist Magazines from the Newport Chartist website archive.

Gwent Local History: The Journal of Gwent Local History Council Editions of 1985 and 2014.

James, Les, *The Struggle for the Charter*: A Newport Museum and Art Gallery Information Sheet (1973).

Osmond, David, *The Chartists 150th Anniversary: A Guided Walk through Newport, Scene of the Chartist Uprising of 1839* (1989) Central, Press, Newport – Pamphlet.

Newport Local History News: *Chartist Special* (1986).

Newspapers

Bristol Mercury.

Bristol Times and Mirror.

The Cambrian.

Cardiff and Merthyr Guardian and Glamorgan, Monmouthshire and Brecon Gazette.

Champion and Weekly Herald.

Monmouthshire Beacon.

Monmouthshire Merlin.

Morning Chronicle.

Northern Liberator.

Northern Star.

Southern Star.

Silurian.

Times.

Usk Observer.

Western Vindicator.

Novels

Austen, Jane, *Emma* (1815).

Dickens, Charles, *Pickwick Papers* (1835).

Dickens, Charles, *Oliver Twist* (1838).

Disraeli, Benjamin, *Sybil*, (1845).

Dickens, Charles, *Little Dorrit* (1855).

Bronte, Charlotte, *Villette* (1855).

Bronte, Charlotte, *The Professor* (1857).

Eliot. George, (Mary Ann Evans), *Middlemarch* (1871).

Websites

About Bristol: *about-bristol.co.uk*

Ancestry: *ancestry.com*

BBC History: *bbc.co.uk/history*

Bristol and Region Archaeological Services: *baras.org.uk*

British Newspaper Archive: *britishnewspaperarchive.co.uk*

Chartism in Newport: *thechartists.org*

Find My Past: *findmypast.co.uk*

General Records Office: *gro.gov.uk*

Gwent Archives: *gwentarchives.gov.uk*

Historic England: *historicengland.org.uk*

Monmouthshire Baptisms and Marriages: *familysearch.org*

Newport Past: *newportpast.com*

Our Chartist Heritage: *our-chartist-heritage.co.uk*

The British Library: *bl.uk*

The Chapels Society: *chapelssociety.org.uk*

The 'Chartist Trials' papers: *chartist.cynefin.wales*

The National Archives: *nationalarchives.gov.uk*

The Peoples Collection Wales: *peoplescollection.wales*

Welsh Newspapers Online: *llgc.org.uk*

Wikipedia: *wikipedia.org*

Notes

1 *Bristol Mercury* 26th October 1844.
2 On her 1851 census form Mary states she was born in Monmouthshire. Her birth year is on her gravestone. There were a number of baby girls named Mary Morgan baptised in Monmouthshire in that year and the following year or two but no conclusive evidence, sadly, whether one of them was Mary.
3 There is a slim file with information on William Foster in Newport Reference Library.
4 The biographical data in this book has been obtained online from: Ancestry, Find My Past and Family Search.
5 A very full biography of William was written by David Mills in 2015. See Sources.
6 National Archives Index to Death Duties IR27/19/2.
7 *Charter* 29th December 1839.
8 Derrick Cyril Vaughan *Newport First Stop* 1990 newportpast.com
9 A copy of William Foster's will is held in Newport Reference Library.
10 I have used the currency converter on the National Archives website for all the money mentioned in this book.
11 *Western Vindicator* 22nd June 1839.
12 The British Library: Discovering Literature *bl.uk*
13 *Charter* 29th December 1839.
14 *Pigot & Co Directory of Monmouthshire* 1822.
15 The 1841 census shows the daughters of William Townsend, John's friend, were in a boarding school in Swansea.
16 *Pigot & Co Directory of Monmouthshire 1822* The shop is described as a 'Linen and Woollen Draper'.
17 *Pigot & Co Directory of Herefordshire and Monmouthshire 1830.*
18 *Cambrian* 29th August 1829.
19 *Cheltenham Chronicle* 3rd September 1829.
20 National Archives Index to Death Duties IR27/214.
21 *Cambrian* 16th October 1830.
22 *Pigot & Co Directory of Herefordshire and Monmouthshire 1830.*
23 Alan Roderick *A Newport Kaleidoscope* 1994 Handpost Books.

24 The area where Friars Walk is now situated.

25 Hadyn Davis, *The History of the Borough of Newport* (1998) Pennyfarthing Press, Newport.

26 *Monmouthshire Merlin* 29th October 1831.

27 *Bristol Mercury*, 2nd March 1833.

28 Chris Evans *Slave Wales: The Welsh and Atlantic Slavery 1660-1850*, University of Wales Press (2010).

29 *Monmouthshire Merlin* 1st December 1838.

30 *Glamorgan, Monmouthshire and Brecon Gazette and Merthyr Guardian* 3rd September 1836.

31 J W Dawson, *Commerce and Custom: A History of the Ports of Newport and Caerleon,* R H Johns 1932.

32 The bills were discovered in 1950 and quoted by Hadyn Davis in *The History of the Borough of Newport.*

33 *Monmouthshire Merlin* 21st December 1839.

34 *Monmouthshire Merlin* 1st July 1837.

35 *Star of Gwent* 2nd February 1861.

36 *Glamorgan, Monmouthshire and Brecon Gazette* and *Merthyr Guardian* 21st and 28th July 1838.

37 David J V Jones, *The Last Rising: The Newport Insurrection of 1839* (1985) Clarendon Press.

38 *Monmouthshire Merlin* 3rd November 1838.

39 *Western Vindicator*, 23rd March 1839.

40 Jutta Schwarzkopf, *Women in the Chartist Movement* (1991) Macmillan.

41 *Monmouthshire Merlin* 13th April 1839.

42 Jutta Schwarzkopf, *Women in the Chartist Movement* (1991) Macmillan.

43 Malcolm Chase, *Chartism a New History* (2007) Manchester University Press.

44 *Western Vindicator*, 16th March 1839.

45 Statement by Rev M Coles, examining magistrate, 11th November 1839 the 'Chartist Trials' papers *www.chartist.cynefin.wales*

46 *Western Vindicator*, 30th March 1839.

47 *London Gazette* July 1837.

48 That he was a Conservative is stated in the account of the Queen's Proclamation in *Monmouthshire Merlin* 1st July 1837. Also he attended the April Anti-Chartist meeting *Monmouthshire Merlin* 13th April 1839.

49 Letter written in London 20th March, *London Evening Standard* 2nd March 1839.

50 David Williams, *John Frost: A Study in Chartism* (1939) University of Wales Press Cardiff.

[51] *Sussex Advertiser*, 22nd May 1826.

[52] *London Courier and Evening Gazette*, 9th July,1831.

[53] *Chelmsford Chronicle*, 4th March 1836.

[54] *Monmouthshire Merlin*, 30th July 1836, 30th September 1837, 16th March 1839.

[55] *Glamorgan, Monmouthshire and Brecon Gazette and Merthyr Guardian*, 23rd March 1839.

[56] In the letter John wrote from Stroud on 2nd April he describes his view of the hills of Monmouthshire and his thoughts of his happy home. *The Charter* 7th April 1839.

[57] *Western Vindicator*, 30th March 1839.

[58] *Western Vindicator*, 6th April 1839.

[59] *Monmouthshire Merlin* 20th April 1839.

[60] *Monmouthshire Merlin* 4th May 1839.

[61] Ivor Wilks *South Wales and the Rising of 1839* (1984) Croon Helm 1984.

[62] *Monmouthshire Merlin* 27th April 1839.

[63] David J V Jones, *The Last Rising: The Newport Insurrection of 1839* (1985) Clarendon Press.

[64] *Chartist Magazine* September 2014.

[65] *Western Vindicator* 25th May 1839.

[66] *Northern Star* 31st August 1839.

[67] *Monmouthshire Merlin* 17th August 1839.

[68] Our Chartist Heritage *www.our-chartist-heritage.co.uk*

[69] *Western Vindicator* 21st September 1839.

[70] *Monmouthshire Merlin* 7th September 1839.

[71] *Northern Star* 28th September 1839.

[72] There are many books and online resources giving facts and theories about the plans, people, routes, motives and outcomes of the Newport Rising. Some are listed at the end of this book.

[73] A full account of William Davies can be found in David Mill's book *William Davies* (2018) Stow Park Printers.

[74] Early readers have told me that the Williams in this account are easily confused. I have therefore listed Mary's family at the beginning of the book.

[75] David J V Jones, *The Last Rising: The Newport Insurrection of 1839* (1985) Clarendon Press.

[76] *Monmouthshire Merlin* 11th January 1840.

[77] The destruction of the Chartist papers is a source of frustration to historians. It would have been marvellous to have had the minutes, etc of the women's meetings.

[78] This area was altered when the railways arrived in Newport and Central Station was constructed.

[79] *Western Mail* 17th March 1877.

[80] David J V Jones, *The Last Rising: The Newport Insurrection of 1839* (1985) Clarendon Press.

[81] The witness statements to the Newport magistrates which record the preliminary hearings in the Westgate Hotel 5th–30th November 1839 are in bound volumes in Newport Reference Library. Amelia's statements are in Volume 3 of the online 'Chartist Trials' transcripts, pages 15-17 *www.chartist.cynefin.wales*

[82] *Monmouthshire Merlin* 7th December 1839.

[83] *Cambrian* 9th November 1839.

[84] *Charter* 17th November 1839.

[85] David J V Jones, *The Last Rising: The Newport Insurrection of 1839* (1985) Clarendon Press.

[86] *Charter* 24th November 1839.

[87] *Northern Liberator* 7th December 1839.

[88] *Northern Star* 30th November 1839.

[89] *Morning Chronicle* 16th December 1839.

[90] *Monmouthshire Merlin* 16th November 1839.

[91] *Champion and Weekly Herald* 24th November 1839.

[92] *Morning Chronicle* 20th December 1839.

[93] *Northern Liberator* 28th December 1839.

[94] *Morning Chronicle* 12th December 1838.

[95] *Northern Star* 7th March 1840.

[96] *Morning Chronicle* 26th December 1839.

[97] The 'Chartist Trials' papers *www.chartist.cynefin.wales*

[98] *Cambrian* 18th January 1840.

[99] *Northern Liberator* 18th January 1840.

[100] *Cambrian* 18th January 1840.

[101] *Cambrian* 18th January 1840.

[102] David J V Jones, *The Last Rising: The Newport Insurrection of 1839* (1985) Clarendon Press.

[103] *Morning Chronicle* 28th January 1840.

[104] *Morning Chronicle* 5th February 1840.

[105] *Southern Star* 9th February 1840.

[106] *Cambrian* 1st February 1840.

[107] *Charter* 9th February 1840.

[108] Home Office file 18/021/00193.

[109] Also in *The Times* 27th February 1840.

[110] *Morning Chronicle* 27th February 1840.

[111] *Northern Star* 14th March 1840.

[112] *Southern Star* 22nd March 1840.

[113] *Northern Star* 29th February 1840.

[114] *Northern Star* 18th April 1840.

[115] *Monmouthshire Merlin* 14th March 1840.

[116] *Cambrian* 7th November 1840.

[117] *Morning Chronicle* 11th November 1840.

[118] *Glamorgan, Monmouthshire and Brecon Gazette and Merthyr Guardian* 1st February 1840.

[119] Advertisements appeared throughout the spring of 1840 in a number of papers offering for sale drawings of John, transcripts of the trial, etc.

[120] *Glamorgan, Monmouthshire and Brecon Gazette and Merthyr Guardian* 7th November 1840.

[121] *Cambrian* 7th November 1840.

[122] *North Wales Chronicle* 10th November 1840.

[123] E.g., *Northern Star* 12th September 1840.

[124] Helen later married and became Mrs Helen Louisa Fruchard. When her first husband died she married again and at this point revealed the identity of her father. Her second marriage took place in 1866 in London and the certificate shows her father to be William Foster Geach, Solicitor.

[125] Malcolm Chase *A Brief History of Chartism*, BBC History Extra, *historyextra.com*

[126] *Western Vindicator* 15th June 1839.

[127] *Northern Star* 25th April 1846.

[128] Malcolm Chase *Chartism a New History* (2007) Manchester University Press.

[129] Ivor Wilks *South Wales and the Rising of 1839* (1984) Croon Helm.

[130] *Northern Star* and *Monmouthshire Merlin* 16th January 1841.

[131] *Bristol Mercury* 16th January 1841.

[132] *Morning Chronicle* 30th January 1841.

[133] *Northern Star* 6th March 1841.

[134] Mary Wright *Montpelier A Bristol Suburb* (2004) Phillimore & Co.

[135] There are good photographs of the row of houses on the Historic England website *historicengland.org.uk*

[136] *Northern Star* 26th June 1841.

[137] *Hereford Journal* 17th March 1841.

[138] Much of the general information about Bristol has come from this guidebook of the time: John Morgan, *A Brief Historical Sketch of Bristol* (1849) H & A Hill, Castle Green.

[139] *Monmouthshire Beacon* 17th April 1841.

[140] *Northern Star* 26th June 1841.

[141] *Bristol Mercury* 25th December 1841.

[142] *Newcastle Journal* Saturday, 15th January 1842.

[143] *Monmouthshire Merlin* 25th December 1841.

[144] *Monmouthshire Beacon* 1st January 1842.

[145] *Morning Advertiser* 29th March 1842.

[146] For information and photos see these websites *about-bristol.co.uk* and *www.wikipedia.org*

[147] Throughout the following month in various papers: *Northern Star*, *Hull Advertiser*, etc.

[148] David Osmond *Newport and the Chartist Land Plan*, *Gwent Local History Journal* (2014).

[149] *Monmouthshire Merlin* 10th September 1842.

[150] *Bristol Mercury* 5th November 1842.

[151] *Monmouthshire Merlin* 21st January 1843.

[152] *Glamorgan, Monmouthshire and Brecon Gazette and Merthyr Guardian* 16th December 1843.

[153] *Monmouthshire Beacon* 29th June 1844.

[154] *Bristol Mercury* 26th October 1844.

[155] *Bristol Mercury* 13th September 1845.

[156] *Bristol Mercury* 14th March 1846.

[157] The record of baptisms and confirmations at St-Mary-on-the-Quay is held in Bristol Archives 37553/R/1/5.

[158] All the petitions from the family and others are in the Home Office Criminal Petitions file H018/21/01.

[159] *Bristol Mercury* 26th November 1853.

[160] *Bristol Mercury* 10th May 1851.

[161] *Morning Advertiser* 14th August 1855.

[162] *Monmouthshire Beacon* 8th July 1854.

[163] David Williams, *John Frost: A Study in Chartism,* (1939) University of Wales Press Cardiff.

[164] *Bristol Times* 22nd February 1851.

[165] Barbara Charlton *Recollections of a Northumbrian Lady 1815 – 1866 ed. L E O Charlton* (1989) Spredden Press.

[166] *Usk Observer* 12th April 1856.

[167] *Usk Observer* 30th August 1856.

[168] *Monmouthshire Beacon* 17th May 1856.

[169] *Monmouthshire Beacon* 19th July 1856.

[170] *Bristol Mercury* 16th August 1856.

[171] Chris Williams, A lecture given at the 2015 Chartist convention in Newport *www.thechartists.org*

[172] James Matthews *Historic Newport* (1910) Williams Press, Newport.

[173] *Usk Observer* 3rd January 1857.

[174] *Bristol Mercury* 19th September 1857.

[175] *Bristol Mercury* 28th November 1857.

[176] *Western Mail* 17th March 1877.

[177] Barbara Charlton *Recollections of a Northumbrian Lady 1815–1866 ed. L E O Charlton* (1989) Spredden Press.

Printed in Great Britain
by Amazon